The Value-driven Project Organisation

JAY ALPHEY

ISBN: 1542703905
ISBN-13: 978-1542703901

Contents

Preface

We read about failing projects every day. Building projects which have gone out of control, IT projects that seem to leave companies in a worse state than they started, change projects which spend money but seem to have no lasting effect. It is easy to see the world of projects as being in crisis. Yet increasingly organisations are delivering value through projects because there are strong perceived benefits to this approach.

This means that more people are involved in projects. Some organisations have put in place individuals with a project title such as "project manager", "program manager", "scrum master" or similar. Some have no such experts with training and time to focus on these skills. And where these experts exist they will be expected to master project management skills, but this does not mean they are the only people to practice them. Effective working within projects requires an understanding of project skills.

These techniques apply at many levels in a project, from a program(me) manager breaking down a multi-year improvement activity into a set of stages which will be implemented as projects, to a team leader working out the best way to structure the work of a small team to deliver their short-term objectives.

The motivation for my books came from my experiences in coaching and training for projects between 2013 and 2016. I was mostly teaching people who hadn't had the opportunity of formal project training before, although many had extensive project experience. The delegates asked me to focus on the key, practical areas which added the most value and so the "Value-driven" approach was born.

About this book

Over the years 1999 to 2016 I held a range of Project Director roles at a UK-based semiconductor company which I will call "ChipCo" to keep it anonymous. Over this time, this grew from a small organisation almost entirely in the UK to a thriving and highly profitable FTSE100 multinational with 30 sites across continents and cultures. I led the program management team in the core semiconductor design business and then owned and developed the corporate approach to project and program management.

We had a challenging project environment. Design cycles might take 2 to 3 years. The designs were innovative Research and Development, but delivered into customer integration projects with tight and fixed schedules. In the semiconductor industry quality is critical. Once your design is "in silicon" and in millions of devices around the world, there are no "second chances".

To address these challenges we developed principles and good practice in project management which helped the company to be hugely successful at on-time, to-quality project delivery. I worked with great teams across many countries, leading and coaching to project success and learning from every interaction.

We are uncovering better ways of developing ...
by doing it and helping others do it

The Agile Manifesto

This book shares some of my learning and experiences about effective project approaches while in these roles. I make no claim to having invented the concepts. Some are classical project management and date back to the mid-20th century. Some have come from the learnings of other companies, especially with the growth of "agile" concepts. Others evolved from the interactions of many teams as we worked out how to solve problems.

There are many books targeted at project practitioners. As project management becomes more widely adopted, books focussed on how to succeed in projects become widespread. There are more than 12000 listed on Amazon at time of writing covering every aspect of project development in domains from construction to behavioural change.

The "Value-driven" series includes two such books. "Value driven Project Planning" (ISBN: 1533059926) and "Value-driven Risk and agility" (ISBN: 1533342008) are aimed at project teams and look at how projects can be planned and run effectively. Like many books in this area, they offer good practice and techniques which have proved effective to project teams.

This book has a different focus. Projects exist in the context of an organisation. To be successful they must deliver value for that organisation. This book explores the "Value-driven" concept from that direction. Rather than looking at how a project team can deliver value, it looks at projects from the viewpoint of the organisation. How can an organisation deliver value through using projects? How can the organisation support the projects to maximise the chance of success?

Acknowledgements

This book is inspired by my own experiences and would never have existed without the talented teams that I have worked with and the constant learnings that I took away from project interactions. I learned something new about projects and teams constantly. I learned even more when I had the chance to sit in another office halfway across the world and work with a team on what we could share and learn from their latest project. My thanks to all of the teams who welcomed me and shared their thinking. It seems almost unfair to single out individuals or groups, but special thanks to a few people at "ChipCo", with no diminishing of my gratitude to others.

To the Austin team for evenings idea-swapping at the Salt Lick and to the Bangalore team for showing me the power and energy of self-belief, to Tudor for reminding me what is on the card, Ken for being honest, John for often seeing it like I do, Shyam for showing me that there is always good beer if you know where to look and to Steve for getting me writing.. And thanks to Paul, Steve, John and Susan for reviewing the book.

More than anyone, my thanks to Liz, Tristan and Jack for making the journey worthwhile.

Examples and principles

Project management is all about practical application. As well as good practice, this book will include some of my own experiences with project planning. We didn't get everything right, but we tried to learn from the mistakes even more than the successes.

Project experiences are shown in the text like this. These are the "narrative" of the book and discuss what I have personally experienced with the teams with which I've worked. Both the good and the less good.

I have always found that others have put key ideas more elegantly than I could hope to do, and in the tradition of "standing on the shoulders of giants" I hope you will find the quotes thought-provoking.

> *Quotes are shown in the text like this.*

Key principles are shown in the text like this.

This book is not intended to be a text book full of problems to wade through. However, this symbol marks suggestions for you could try out for yourself, or to take a break from the book and think about how the subject applies in your own projects. .

Chapter 1

What is "Value-driven"?

High value project activities tend to focus on the project and the people involved. This is typically seen as more important than adherence to standardised rules. There are many specific project methodologies defined for different applications by different groups. These use standardised language, stages, documents and rules and the consistency brings some benefit to an organisation. These include the Bodies of Knowledge (BoKs) from APM (Association for Project Management) and PMI (Project Management Institute), Prince2 and Scrum to name but a few.

It is a bewilderingly large field. Google returns nearly 400,000 hits for "Project Methodology". Wikipedia lists fifteen different international standards. This is without considering the myriad of company-specific approaches.

"Value-driven" project management is not focused on a single approach. There are guides to the details of each specific methodology. In the "Value-driven" project management books I am looking behind the individual rules and exploring why these may add value. You should feel free to pick and choose the best and most applicable parts of different approaches. This may take a little more time and thought than adopting a complete package, but it lets you think about *why* you are following each rule.

> *Do nothing which is of no use.*
>
> *"A book of five rings" Miyamoto Musashi*

Chapter 2

Value and Projects

This book is aimed at organisational leaders. It is not intended to help project teams run projects, although I hope that project teams will also find it useful in thinking about how they fit into the organisation as a whole. It is about how organisations can *use* projects to deliver value. If you are reading this book, you are thinking about how to make your organisation most effective and how projects can help with this.

With any project, I always suggest that you start by visualising what success looks like. What do you want to gain from this book? What is your role within the organisation? What do you see as the challenges for your organisation and where is your role in addressing these? Take a few minutes to note this down before we start.

As a reader, you may be looking at introducing projects into an organisation, or improving organisational capability. You may have a new organisation, a scaleup or an established organisation which wants to increase project capability. Each of these have their challenges as you will be aware. Whatever the circumstances, you have a desire and a need to understand both what makes projects effective and how to get to that end goal.

That's great! Firstly, you are not alone in wanting to make this work. Project management is widespread because it is viewed as an effective approach for delivering organisational goals. Adoption of project management continues to increase and is increasingly seen as a key factor in organisational success.

> *Worldwide, organizations will embrace, value, and utilize project management and attribute their success to it.*
>
> ***Envisioned Goal,. Project Management Institute***

But isn't it easy?

Successful implementation seems to remain a challenge. All too often we are assailed with newspaper headlines reporting failures and overruns. It is easy to ask whether it is even possible to build an effective project based organisation or whether projects are doomed to failure.

Of organisations surveyed...

32% "never or sometimes" complete on time

31% "never or sometimes" deliver full benefit

31% "never or sometimes" complete on budget

46% "never or sometimes" have a track record of success

The state of project management survey 2016
Association for Project Management

It's clear that there are barriers to successful implementation. This survey suggests only a third of organisations have a significant on time project record and half feel they have no track record of success. There are pitfalls in running projects and clearly you are not alone in wondering how to make projects successful.

There is some perception that managing projects is a solved problem. Despite all the evidence that organisations struggle with projects, there is a widespread (but fortunately not universal) belief that managing projects isn't hard. It can be hard to see where this comes from, but it seems to persist even against strong evidence to the contrary.

One CEO that I spoke to was very frustrated because he had asked four different people to set up a project approach in his organisation and they had all failed. Despite the importance of the role, he was convinced this was easy. And because he felt it was easy, he'd asked very junior people to do the job. They had failed because they lacked experience. But because he felt it was easy he felt they were all incompetent, not inexperienced.

Another team that I worked again needed to set up a complete project approach. Their projects were failing to deliver on many measures. They knew that they needed someone to address this. The senior management looked at an experienced candidate to address the problem. They turned him down because he was "just a project management expert". This was an expertise they didn't feel that they needed, despite their intended goals.

A side note about that term "just". I often say "there is no right time to use the word 'just' ". I can picture a few people smiling if they read this. Think about it next time you use the word. Nine times out of ten people say "just" to reduce the perceived value or importance of an skill or activity that they do not themselves have or perform.

There is no shortage of proposed solutions. Specific approaches and methodologies claim to achieve easy and effective project delivery. There are now a huge selection of competing ideas. Some are driven by individuals or organisations. Some promote the growing market in project management qualifications or training. Others sell vast manuals containing a "Body of Knowledge". With a wide range of cryptically-named approaches, it is hard for an experienced practitioner to make headway. So how can you steer through this maze to understand how to make your organisation effective?

Figure 1- A montage of methods

Such a range of different approaches and ideas can be disruptive to an organisation. With no overall picture, one group may adopt one approach and another take a different direction. Language usage diverges, ideological disputes occur and the organisation risks getting distracted from the overall objectives. Most people with some background in project management are aware of the long and often bitter arguments between "Waterfall" and "Agile" approaches, even though the terms themselves are so generic and open to interpretation as to make any argument of little value.

In your organisation, how do you run projects? Have you adopted an external standard, or did you build your own approach? Is there one approach or are there many? Do they work effectively together? How does a new person in the organisation know how projects are managed?

The chart below comes from the "State of Scrum" report 2015 from the Scrum Alliance and highlights the level of internal conflict perceived in respondents. Only 20% of those surveyed felt there was no tension between their project approach and the organisation as a whole. So 80% of project teams surveyed are feeling that their way of working doesn't fit comfortably into the organisation. An 80% mismatch suggests something is missing in how organisations fit with projects.

Figure 2- Organisational tension ("State of Scrum" report 2015)

What's in a name? As we started to gain more acceptance of agile working, there was a debate over what we should call the teams working in this way. The organisation had always used sequential planning. We wanted to identify what was different about the new approach. But some teams were trying to follow a specific approach, such as Scrum. They were sticking rigidly to the framework of their chosen methodology. Others were just starting to move down the path towards agile working. They were using some Agile methods but in a more experimental way.

What was wrong with saying "we use Scrum"? We had some expert teams, some early adopters and some using other approaches. The name couldn't really apply to all groups. As often happens, language had started to become a barrier.

In the end we looked for common ground. There was one common factor between all of the teams. All the agile teams used iterative planning. They split the project into stages (iterations, sprints or timeboxes according to the naming of your approach). So we used "Iterative" to descibe this way of working.

Everyone was broadly happy with the name. This worked effectively as an envelope. When we talked about "how does iterative development fit into our processes?" everyone knew what we meant. And all the teams involved felt included and able to contribute.

Moving forwards

This book is intended to help you move forwards. It is not trying to "teach" project management or a specific approach. As a result it will not go into detail about specifics of one way of working or another way. You will need to make choices about what approach you use and you will find some guidance here but you will need more detailed training and reference for project teams when you decide the approach. But as a leader you need to understand what you can expect from projects and how to make that expectation real. You need to build an approach to project management that enables good teams who produce value for the business.

This book is about how to ensure that your organisational strategy is well connected to project implementation. We can view the organisation as a building. If we want a strategy that enables value for the organisation we need a good foundation in the ability of projects to deliver. Projects are the engine which will generate value for the organisation.

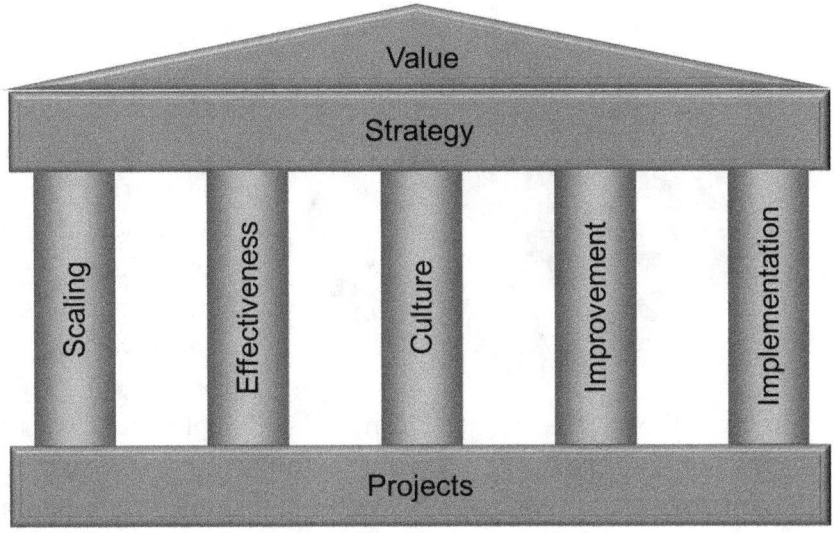

Figure 3- Integrating projects to strategy

The book will look at the way that the projects connect to the strategy and so deliver value. These are the pillars in the picture above. The book looks at key areas joining projects to strategy:

Scaling
- How does the organisation grow and how does this affect the relationship with projects?

Effectiveness
- How can you join the projects to the organisation as an effective whole?

Culture
- How does a "project organisation" ensure that the project teams build value?

Improvement
- How can you learn and develop as an organisation?

Implementation
- How can you get the organisation to where you want to be?

Methodologies come and go, but teams are always at the heart of projects. In the ancient Egyptian tomb of Menkaure there is a piece of graffiti left there by a team working on the construction project. This team refer to themselves as the "Drunkards of Menkaure". The ideas in this book are part of a chain of learning of effective approaches which stretches back to the dawn of time and the earliest human endeavours. I like to think of the "Drunkards of Menkaure" cheering me on and raising another glass as I write.

Chapter 3

Responding to growth

This book is about change. You want to change the approach that your organisation is taking to projects. And you want to change for a reason. Perhaps you feel you should be able to do better – deliver more and faster. Most likely there is a sound business reason driving your need for improvement. And the explanation is likely to be centred around organisational change.

Organisations are not static. They are formed, they grow and develop, expand, acquire, change markets, stagnate and even die. And every change in the organisation drives changing needs. The approaches that were right for your organisation last year will not necessarily be the right ones for you next year.

Think about your own organisation. How long has it been in existence? How is it growing or developing? And what about the group to which you belong within the organisation? Do you see tensions from changes as the organisation grows and shifts focus?

To understand the organisational needs for project management we need to understand organisations and how they evolve. As we look around organisations it seems clear, at least anecdotally, that smaller organisations tend not to use formal project management approaches.

Larger organisations seem increasingly to see projects as a structured approach that is valuable to achieve goals. So project management adoption seems to increase with organisational size.

The contrasts are clearest with small groups integrated into larger organisations. I worked with a number of smaller groups or acquisitions where I was helping the group to integrate. It was very clear that the project management approaches which the larger organisation saw as normal were initially viewed by the smaller groups as threatening. This seemed an inevitable consequence of the difference in sizes. The scale was clearly leading to very different viewpoinst.

This difference is evident in many studies. The data below is based on organisations who have implemented a Project Management Office (PMO), which as we will see is an accepted mechanism for delivering project structure into the organisation. Smaller organisations than those in this survey would presumably have a lower adoption rate.

Mid-size and large companies are far more likely to have a PMO than small companies

The State of Project Portfolio Management 2014
PM Solutions

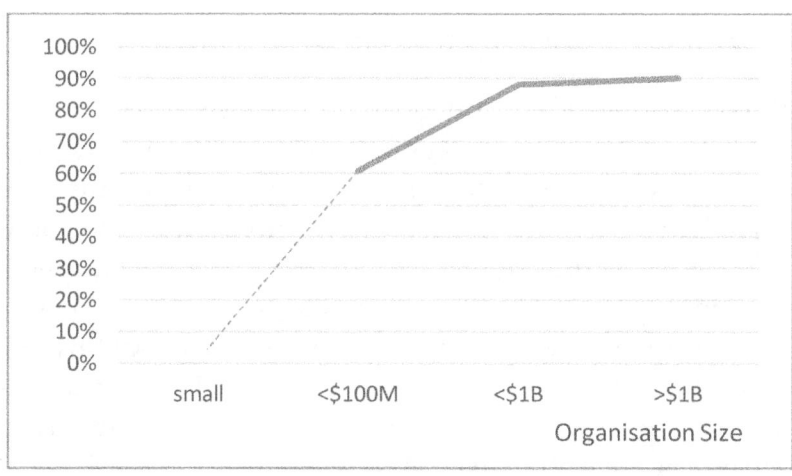

Figure 4- Adoption of a Project Management Office

Organisational growth model

We see a difference in attitude to projects between small and large organisations. Formal approaches and Project Management Offices seem to be a feature of larger organisations. Smaller organisations seem to lack these structures. Most people would see this as "natural" (or at least matching their own experiences). To understand this and to explore the effect of growth on project approaches, we need to think about how organisations grow. It seems that an organisation does not start with structured projects in mind. So at what point does the mindset shift and formalising projects become attractive? And why does this occur?

There are several models for organisational growth. As with all models, naming differences and detailed interpretation vary somewhat. However the broad picture of how an organisation evolves is fairly well agreed. A simple lifecycle model might be as below, where the curve measures a meaningful output parameter, such as total revenue or other generated output. Revenue starts low and flat as the company finds its market, grows as the business model becomes successful and penetrates the market, flattens as the market starts to saturate or competition increases, and finally declines if the market changes or disruptive competitors appear.

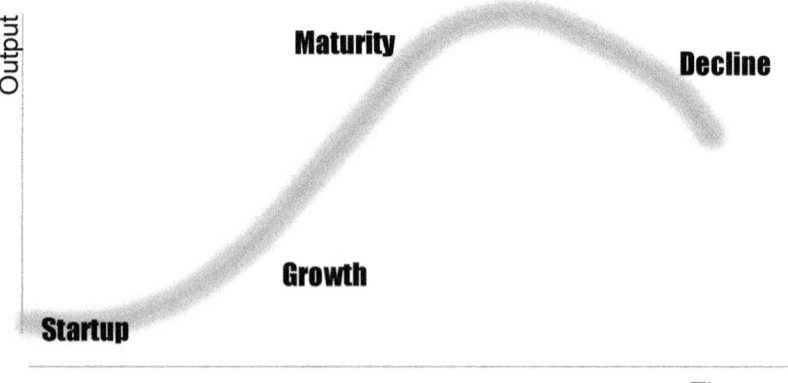

Figure 5- Simple lifecycle model

This model isn't nearly detailed enough for our needs. A mature organisation has probably already matured its processes and defined its approaches.   There may be subsequent changes, perhaps due to a modified market or to avoid the "Decline" stage. But the bulk of the change and development around the approach to projects occurs in those earlier growth stages. We will need to focus in on those earlier stages to try to understand what is changing, beyond the visible increase in revenue. And we also need to think about what the drivers are at each stage which are changing the approach to projects. Size and revenue are factors, but there is more involved in the approach and structure of the organisation.

A classic model for organisational growth was created by Greiner. This was described in his 1972 article "Evolution and Revolution as Organisations Grow". Although the article is nearly 50 years old, I still find it an insightful read.   Greiner suggests that organisations progress through plateau states with characteristics of behaviour and structure.   In between these states (the "Evolution" stages of the title) are transitions (the "Revolutions") when the organisation reaches a "crisis" and needs to make a radical change. Each organisation, Greiner suggests, transitions through these stages, and each plateau state has its own approach to managing the business.   Indeed semi-autonomous groups within an organisation may also exhibit similar stages within the overall lifecycle of the organisation. Growth and change affect the nature of the problems and solutions which the project organisation must address.

> *Managerial problems and practices are rooted in time.*
> *They do not last throughout the life of an organization*
>
> *"Evolution and Revolution as Organisations Grow" Greiner*

Greiner's model proposes the organisational stages below. I have summarised these briefly, although I'd recommend the original paper if you want more details. Each stage is an evolution of the organisation with its own approach, and each faces its own problems and eventual revolutionary transition. As you see the organisation reshaping through these stages you can appreciate how this will affect project approaches in the organisation.

Creativity Stage

This stage is focussed on creating a product and a market. Internally here are frequent, informal communication methods. The organisation is very responsive to customer responses, leading to short term planning focus.

The stage ends in the "Crisis of Leadership". The need for management increases, while the current leaders may have skills and interest more aligned with technology.

Direction Stage

The organisation starts to build functional structure, separating marketing from production. Accounting systems and budgeting are introduced. Organisational hierarchy appears.

This leads to the "Crisis of Autonomy". The leaders have become separated from the lower level employee, with the leaders continuing to be directive but understanding the details less well.

Delegation Stage

The organisational structure becomes decentralised with more local responsibility. Management by exception becomes the normal approach and senior management communication is far less frequent.

This ends in a "Crisis of Control". Top management seeks to regain control over an organisation which has become diverse. But central management cannot cope with the diversity.

Coordination Stage

Formal systems and approaches are introduced into the organisation to increase co-ordination. This may include planning approaches and formalised profit and loss groupings. Some data management becomes centralised, while decentralised operation remains the normal approach.

This leads to the "Crisis of Red Tape". Bureaucracy increases as centralised rules become increasingly burdensome and removed from day-to-day functions.

Collaboration Stage

Strong interpersonal interactions start to replace formal process and systems. Teams become increasingly self-governing and work independently on a project basis. Education, information systems and discussion become the key tools to ensuring consistency.

We can see that this model suggests radical transformations over the life of a growing organisation. And these changes will change the need and the application of project management. As Greiner's naming is quite specific to his topic, I have shown the stages below with more generic names which I will refer to in the rest of the book.

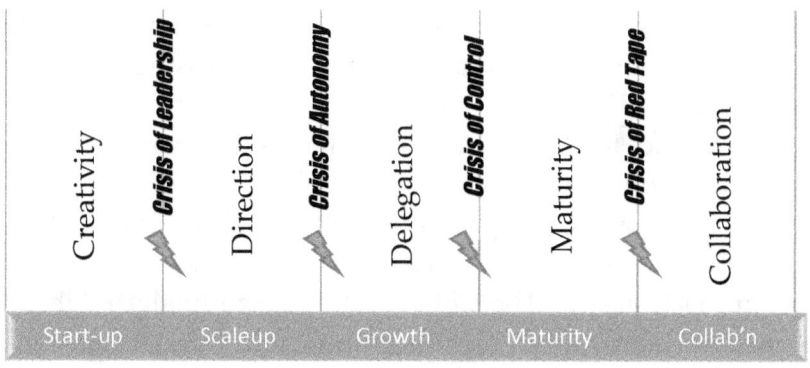

Figure 6- Organisational growth stages

> *Where do you see your organisation or group in the*
> *Greiner model? Are you a new start-up in an initial*
> *creative stage? Or perhaps an established organisation*
> *struggling to loosen the red tape and become more open*
> *and collaborative?*

So how might these changes be affecting some of the key factors in project management? Let's look at some of these factors and think about how these may develop through the organisational lifecycle. Rather than looking stage by stage I have pulled out some key topics and we can look at how these might typically evolve.

Project Planning

In the early stages of the organisation, predictability is low. There is little past history to use in planning. Technology is challenging and problems may be hard to predict and anticipate. And it is necessary to respond fluidly to customer requests. All of these factors tend to promote a low level of planning initially and a highly responsive or reactive organisation.

With budgeting appearing at the Scaleup stage, we grow the need to predict and measure cost to ensure that the growing business can afford and track the work. The Growth stage brings in more exception management as a control technique. This links to the use of plans as tracking mechanisms. Management can only assess if a project is "on track" by having a plan against which to track, so planning becomes a key tool for assessing and managing progress. The Maturity stage will tend to introduce formalised approaches to planning in which the teams are trained. This could include consistent approaches for planning, plan templating and the use of good practice methods such as Critical Path Management, Earned Value or Story Points (according to the approach used). The Collaboration stage finally might bring in wider collaborative planning approaches and extensive use of historic data and project lessons.

Project Control Systems

If we look at tools and systems, we see a similar profile. Initially project control will be through oversight by a small number of individuals, through discussion rather than formal tools. The Scaleup stage will tend to bring in cost controls and approval, although probably manually and not through integrated tooling. The Growth stage will need to introduce mechanisms to support exception management, which probably needs approval and gating approaches. By the Maturity stage, the scale is sufficient that formal tools are needed and there is likely to be an explosion of tools and control points. This is then slightly relaxed in favour of expert judgement as we enter the final Collaboration stage.

The profile of project management usage will typically be similar to the diagram below: The solid line represents the investment on Planning approaches and tends to increase in a more mature organisation. Planning will typically become more complex and integrated with the need to plan at project, programme and portfolio levels as the organisation grows. The dashed line shows effort invested in processes and controls. This will typically increase in the early stages as the organisation stabilises. It will then fall off slightly after the Crisis of Red Tape as the teams start to self-organise more and rely on personal skills more than imposed structure.

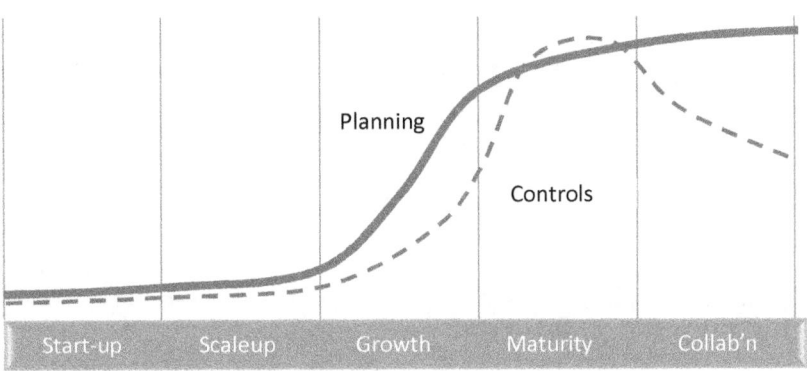

Figure 7- Project approaches through organisational stages

From my own experience, the transition that occurs at the growth phase can be hard to manage. The stage is characterised by new challenges, new customers and a change of scale. At the same time, formal approaches to project management are being applied. Everyone is running to scale last year's approaches so they don't break as the organisation scales. It's a challenge to get people to think ahead to "what we will need" rather than "what will get us working right now".

I was talking about scaling to a VP of Project Planning in a mid-sized organisation. I raised the problem of transitioning towards stability and away from crisis management. There was a long pause and he replied "That would be amazing. I don't think I've ever worked anywhere that isn't 100% in crisis mode". Escaping this trap is a stage in organisational maturity, not necessarily linked to a specific organisational size. In this case, although the organisation was no longer small, it was still in many ways trapped in a reactive mode of operation.

Need/supply model

There's a slightly simpler way to look at the organisational change. We have seen that the need for project process varies with the organisational maturity. The capability to supply process also varies. An organisation can be categorised by both the need and supply of project process. "Need" represents how much the organisation needs defined processes in order to function, while "supply" is its ability to generate appropriate processes to address that need. In this model we can characterise organisations into four categories. An organisation will transition through these as in the chart below.

Low need/Low supply

In the initial stages, the organisation typically lacks the skills to define processes in an effective way. It also does not have an immediate need for formal project management approaches. The focus is short term and the activities may not be repeatable. Dealing with immediate problems is likely to dominate. Project processes are likely to be lightweight and should be so.

High need/Low supply

In the Growth stage there starts to be a significant need for a more rigorous approach to cover the scaling of people and complexity. However the organisation has no history of project management. It probably lacks the skills and with needs changing fast it can be very challenging to develop the approaches needed. Typically the organisation responds by putting team members into project management roles. The outcome is generally a simple project approach which functions adequately but which is specific to the current circumstances. This can be hard to develop and extend and probably does not use much learning from external good practice.

High need/High supply

By the Maturity stage it is critical for the business to have stable and repeatable ways of working. Processes become critical to enable reliable delivery and as the organisation stabilises, there is more focus on project management as a means to repeatable success. By this point experienced project managers have been appointed or developed and a scalable process is likely to have been developed which has survived the organisational growth.

Low need/High supply

Project processes are in place and well understood. The focus shifts to continuous improvement owned by practitioners rather than imposed rules. The organisation has experienced teams and project managers but may be hitting the Crisis of Red Tape. It must adapt to a more collaborative approach and find a balance between process and collaboration which is effective and may be hard to find.

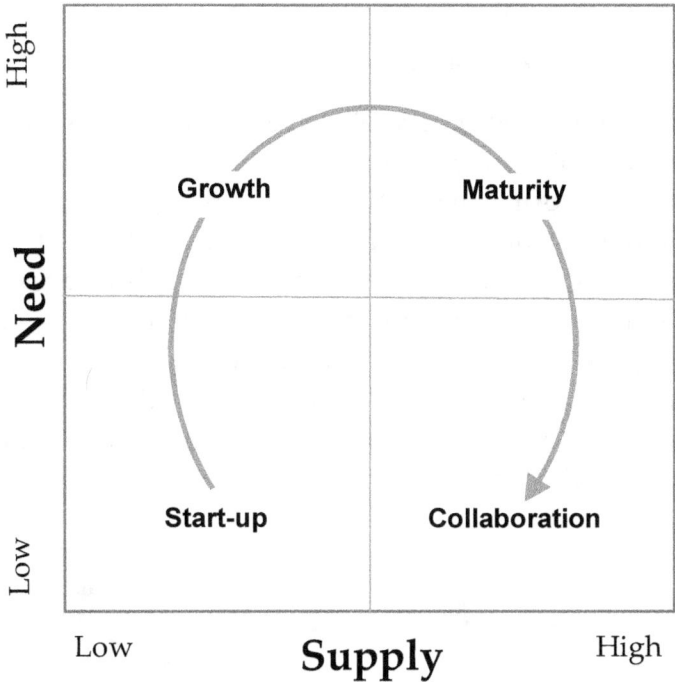

Figure 8- Transition through the Supply/Need curve

 How does this map to your organisation? How much capability to supply project guidance do you have? And how much need? In terms of balance do you feel you are under- or over-supplied?

Impact of scaling

Scaling Project Communication

Project communication varies hugely with project scale. In a small project, typical of a small organisation, communication is generally informal and between individuals. Every team member talks to every other team member as and when is needed. This approach is very effective, but scales poorly. With a team of 4 there are 6 possible communication paths, which is quite easy to manage. With a team of 8 this has increased to 28 paths. With 50 people it is over 1200. This issue is worsened because the 4 people may be in one room, the team of 8 in one building, and the team of 50 in several countries and time zones.

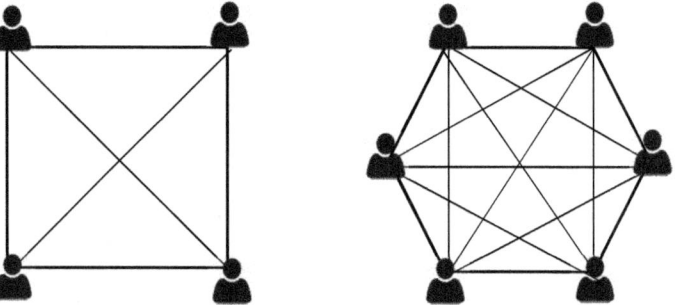

Figure 9- Increasing communication paths with scaling

Small teams often rely on information exchange within the group. This ensures that everyone is working from the same "version of the truth". As the team grows, ensuring consistency of approach and understanding becomes harder. Knowledge becomes localised and ceases to be automatically shared.

Scaling begins to require mechanisms to be built to exchange data. These mechanisms require process rules and data formats and locations. With any increased team size, there is a limit to the usage of any approach which relies on informal verbal communication and knowledge sharing within the group.

The growing organisation typically groups projects into teams and sub teams. Communication within a team continues freeform, while between the teams it is managed. This is generally either through a manager/facilitator or through agreed peer-to-peer contacts. The "manager" approach can lead to a "silo'd" system. If all communication between groups is channelled through managers, the communication may be influenced by differing opinions and objectives on the project. The peer-to-peer approach is a standard solution when scaling Agile teams. In an approach like Scrum, which is built on informal knowledge sharing, scaling rapidly becomes a problem. The most widely adopted approach is for each team to have their internal communication or "Scrum", with each of these delegating a representative to a larger team, called a "Scrum of Scrums".

> *Any team over 7 in size should be split up*
> *into multiple SCRUMs.*
>
> *Jeff Sutherland, Scrum Inc*

I should maybe say something about Agile and specifically Scrum at this point. In this book, I'm not looking in detail at any specific methodology. However Agile is a new area to many people and I have already mentioned Scrum. Communication is a key part of Agile in general and of Scrum in particular. Many of the great ideas in Agile come out of building on the power of communication within small flexible teams. In many ways, this is developing the same ideas that make start-ups successful – small, focussed teams working together on a shared goal. The communication barriers that challenge growing organisations are the same as challenge growing Agile teams. As Agile matures and its approaches become accepted for small teams, there is a fascinating on-going debate on how you scale this without losing the benefits.

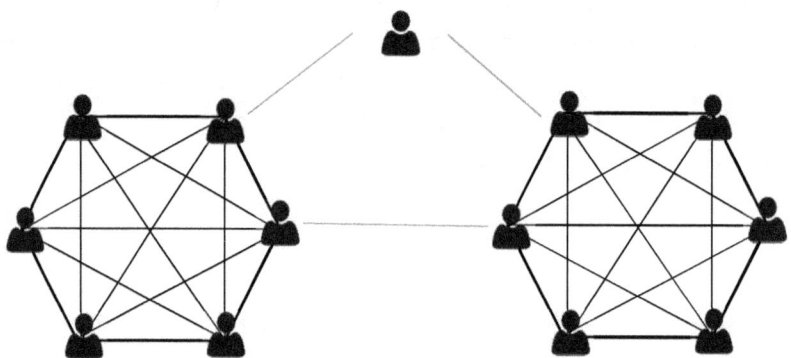

Figure 10- Managing communication paths in larger organisations

This approach allows significant scaling. Although there is no absolute figure for optimum team size, the rapid increase in communication paths, coupled with the difficulty of co-locating large teams within speaking distance, typically leads to teams working optimally between 5 and 10 people. This represents quite a wide range of between 10 and 45 communication paths.

A project of up to 100 could be managed with a single level of hierarchy. It would be split into 5 to 10 sub teams of 5 to 10 people, each delegating one person to an oversight team. The sub teams are then of a manageable scale and can be co-located to maximise the efficiency of communication within the team. This fits quite closely with the general advice for Agile teams of limiting team size to around 7 people.

This approach is often referred to as a "cellular" project organisation. The teams form tight "cells" which communicate well internally. But potentially you build challenging communications between cells as in the diagram below. Scaling needs to consider the different distances of communication and the challenges which these introduce.

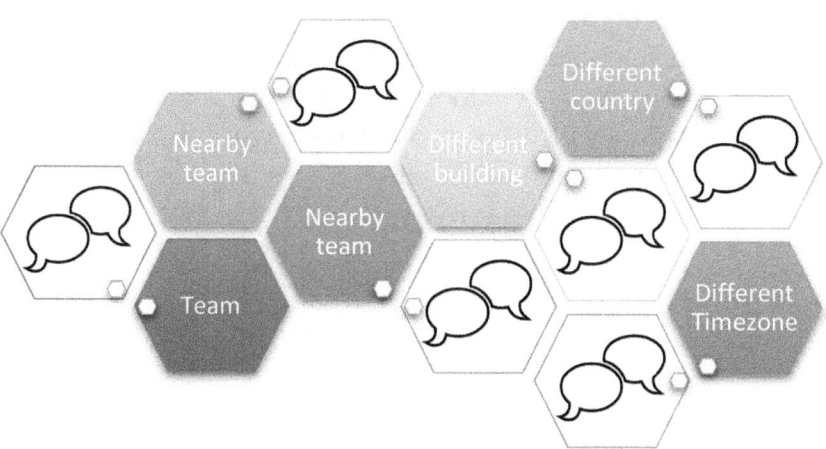

Figure 11- Communication in the cellular organisation

The cellular organisation introduces far more process needs. The sub teams need to be able to export and import information between teams. This implies data and reporting needs. And to transfer knowledge rather than only data suggests compatible formats. The teams must work in a relatively aligned way. The oversight team must have a structure and an approach. There will be training needs to ensure the approach is understood. There may be compliance and audit needs to ensure that the approach is applied effectively and avoids conflict or dominance issues. The culture must be very supportive of cross-team working.

This is especially true if one sub-team is at a different site, and represented in the top-level meeting by one individual, probably on a phone line. In this situation, information transfer can be poor and the remote team may easily become isolated. In some organisations the remote team may become a "scapegoat" who are blamed for failure. This can especially be a problem if the remote team are (as is often the case) a group which are late in the development chain with significant dependencies. This could be a testing, support, documentation or similar group. The organisation will need to be inclusive and low-blame to ensure accurate information is revealed.

How well do cross site meetings work? Have you had reviews with some of the team on the phone? Maybe from a different country, with a different timezone and even a different language? How many problems have you seen set up because of lack of effective inter-team communication?

Organisational scaling was a key issue at ChipCo. Initially the organisation was built on tight, co-located teams in a single room. This was very effective for increasing speed and reducing errors. But as teams grew from five to 50 or more, and spread across multiple continents, the projects became much harder to run. The approach had to be modified. Typically each team would have one or more engineering leads and the team leads would collectively make project decisions. This is similar to the "Scrum of Scrums" concept but would typically involve project and commercial management in the meetings as well as technical peers.

We did find representation of remote teams to be a problem. Some teams were unwilling to raise issues. In particular where a team was represented by a manager, they might minimise issues to appear more in control. Or they might be concerned about seeming less knowledgeable or experienced. Skilled meeting facilitators helped, as these could ensure everyone stayed involved and contributing. The key factor was a long programme of building a project culture where raising, not hiding, issues was accepted and expected.

Scaling Project Risk management

Organisational scaling also affects the balance between creativity and delivery. A start-up is typically focussed primarily on solving the challenges of making the outcomes work at all. The small organisation is focussed on opportunity – how it can exploit its assets. It can (and usually must) take risks to address a new market. Through the organisational lifecycle, repeatable delivery becomes more critical. A large organisation needs to deliver reliably on promises. This sees a shift in risk profile in the organisation. A higher focus on Risk leads to a higher need for many project management functions. Reliable planning becomes key to understanding what is achievable. Reporting status and identifying future problem areas allows the business to respond flexibly.

Not only is the organisation becoming more wary of Risk, but the areas of Risk will be changing. In smaller projects and organisations, failures of construction are often dominant. This is where technical complexity, limited experience or new environments cause the implementation of a project to fail. The team is focussed on solving today's crises for the good reason that these are the key failure points.

As the project grows, the causes of failure change. Errors in prediction begin to outweigh errors in action. With a more complex project environment, more stakeholders and more interactions, we see more failures due to that complexity. This might be an error in design, where the wrong approach is taken to solve a problem. Or it could often be an error in requirements, where the problem is not correctly identified, or a key component of the problem is missed. Or a failure in planning so that an approach cannot be followed, a key dependency is missed or an unanticipated risk impacts the project. In this environment individual skills are no longer sufficient to recover or prevent failure and good practice approaches need to be adopted.

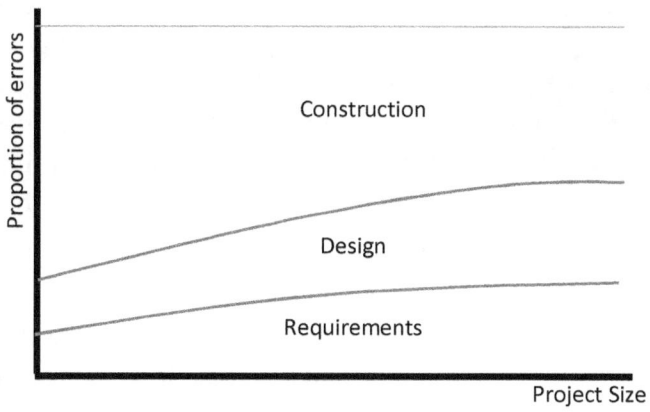

Figure 12- Sources of project error (after Capers Jones)

Chapter 4

Building the culture

As a leader, your role is to set a direction for the organisation. You rely on others to deliver the steps along that path. This book assumes you will be using projects as the mechanism for delivering the strategy. We will look at a model that can be used to formalize and regulate the linkage of the strategy to the delivery. But there can still be a disconnect in the organisation between strategy and implementation.

It's not enough to define an approach for delivery through projects. The success or failure of an organisation will be down to whether the approach is effective. If not, the strategy risks becoming a set of desires disconnected from the reality "on the ground". This is sometimes referred to as "ivory tower" strategy planning due to the separation between the strategic management and the project implementation. The separation may be physical, with the management offices physically separated from the project teams, but more critically there may be a divide in way of thinking which prevents the projects from being effective.

How effective is your organisational culture? Are the plans made at a strategic level converted to effective activities? Think about what barriers there are. What behaviours in the organisation are acting for or against the effective delivery of strategy as projects?

When strategy becomes separated from an organisation's ability to deliver, the strategy is not the winner.

Address culture before process

What if the organisation is not implementing your strategy effectively? It's frustrating for you as the leader. How do you respond? Well, once the organisation has reached a certain scale, it has a defined set of approaches to implement projects. This would typically be by the end of the Growth stage in our lifecycle model. If you have a defined approach to projects, then perhaps you feel that supplying more detail, more rules and checks, will ensure compliance to the rules and so ensure successful project delivery.

This is a fairly common response. It is emphasized by the nature of the people involved in defining the project approach. Through the Growth stage and into Maturity the organisation has been appointing people to develop process. Their role and purpose is to constrain and direct the organisation. Not unnaturally they respond to a problem by increasing the constraints. The risk is that you have a "run-away" increase in detailed application of process. This is the risk area that we highlighted as the "Crisis of Red Tape".

> *The Crisis of Red Tape: Procedures take precedence over problem solving, and innovation dims. In short, the organization has become too large and complex to be managed through formal programs and rigid systems.*
>
> *Greiner - Evolution and revolution as organizations grow*

How then do we reach the final lifecycle stage of a Collaborative organisation? If the path there is not through increasing the defined process, then what do we use?

> *If you want to build a ship, don't drum up the men to gather wood, divide the work and give orders.*
> *Instead, teach them to yearn*
> *for the vast and endless sea.*
> *As for the future, your task is not to foresee it,*
> *but to enable it*
>
> *Antoine de Saint-Exupery*

We need an alternative mechanism that is not derived from externally applied rules. It's not immediately obvious what this would be, which is why organisations do fall back on increased process. Greiner proposes what he terms "Social control" as the approach. But how does "Social control" work and how can we ensure that it moves the organisation in the direction that we want it to head? We will explore this by looking at the idea of "Project Culture".

> *Social control and self-discipline replace formal control. This transition is especially difficult for the experts who created the coordination systems as well as for the line managers who relied on formal methods for answers.*
>
> *Greiner - Evolution and revolution as organizations grow*

The "crisis of red tape" can be hard for managers. In a growing organisation they are pushing ways of working, frameworks, checks, metrics and measures. Now a rapid shift in thinking is needed. You need individual competency within the framework, collaboration, shared good practice and coaching.

I remember one team which were very technology-led and completely resistant to project approaches. I worked with them for two years, bringing in good practices when I could show benefit and always feeling that I was pushing a rock uphill. But after two years we were aligned. They understood that the approaches we had introduced were protecting them from failed projects, not preventing them from doing good work.

At that point it would have been so easy to keep pushing because that was what I was used to. By good fortune I was on a long-running coaching course at the time and this gave me the motivation to step back, stop the pressure and move to a coaching approach.

Some managers visibly kept pushing process detail. Generally they became very focused on compliance measures. Unfortunately, this tended to push their teams towards avoiding apparent failure rather than increasing success.

What is "Project Culture"?

What is "culture"? What does "culture" mean when applied to projects? If culture is a key factor in the evolved organisation, how do we ensure that the culture is beneficial to achieving your goals?

> *Culture - The attitudes and behaviour characteristic of a particular social group*
>
> ***Oxford English Dictionary***

Culture is about what a group or team considers "normal" behaviour. In the absence of alternative guidance, teams will always follow their own normal practice, and so be steered by their cultural norms. Project teams may have documented and agreed processes to guide them. Teams can always ask for advice from outside the team. But however detailed the support on offer, they will have to make some decisions and judgement calls on their own. More experienced and competent teams will generally make more independent decisions. As the organisation grows, autonomy must grow also - a single leader can no longer direct the whole organisation. This means that experienced teams will rely heavily on their own internal model in making choices and progressing their work.

So, what if the organisational culture is not a match to the intended objectives? The symptoms will become obvious. The teams, when left alone, are making decisions which do not match the desires of the company management. Perhaps the projects are not effective at delivering value. Inevitably there will be a conflict between the implementation teams and the strategy development management. The company may fail to achieve the intended objectives. Or the management may respond with a heavy-handed "command and control" approach. Here the management tries to take every decision away from the project team, driving the "Crisis of Red Tape" situation. The organisation becomes slow and unable to scale. And the situation becomes very demoralising to the teams. Low morale may lead to increased separation between teams and management, increasing the problems.

Figure 13- Bad cultural reinforcement

Figure 14- Good cultural reinforcement

To build a "project culture" in an organisation can be a substantial change in behaviour. The team have their existing internal model and changing this will need external direction, guidance and encouragement. However, teams do not only exhibit their "normal" behaviour because of the absence of guidance. They typically resist attempts to change their cultural norms. Culture can be extremely robust and introducing a "project" culture to an organisation can be very challenging. But as the organisation transitions through its growth stage it must be developing a culture which supports project delivery. While a project culture may be unformed in the Startup stage, it is a critical necessity by the later stages of the lifecycle. And behaviours that are widespread and natural in a small team may not scale as the organisation grows without substantial encouragement.

Does culture really make such a difference? The PMI's "Pulse of the Profession" (2015) report rated culture as **the single most significant differentiator** between high and low performing organisations. The difference which this makes is startling. In their data, 80% of high performing organisations were rated with a culture that "fully understand the value of project management". This compares with a figure of only 36% of low performing organisations.

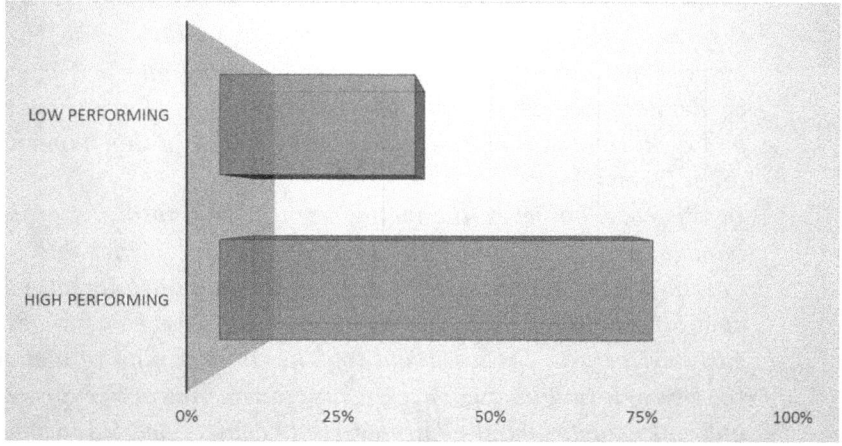

Figure 15- Project culture against organisational performance

Culture will be a key factor in your ability to implement the strategy that you are proposing. Or as Drucker succinctly puts it…

I have worked with teams with very different project cultures. And from this I see culture as a (maybe even "the") key differentiator for project success. This isn't about nationality, although clearly working with distributed multi-national teams is a challenge. Nor is it about communication barriers, although location, time zone, language and media used may all hinder a team's ability to communicate. I often talk with my teams about "honest planning". It's a simple phrase but it's at the heart of what I see as good project culture. Honest planning means that commitments are based on the team's understanding of the project. They input into the process. They are allowed, or rather encouraged, to raise and openly discuss concerns and risks.

A great example of good project culture came in planning a large processor project. The team invested lots of work in the plans, looking at historic data, options for scope and performance and came out with a plan scenario. However, the marketing team felt the resulting plan would be too late to market. The group management might have ignored the planning and just put an earlier date on the roadmap. This would probably have alienated and demotivated the project team (and I've seen this happen in other teams).

In this case, however, the management agreed with the project team a new plan which was aggressive but achievable. It involved some assumptions than the team had initially not been comfortable to plan with. They sold the business benefits of the early delivery to the team and together built a plan to manage the risk of late delivery. This left the team feeling both supported and enthusiastic about what they could achieve and led to a very successful product delivery.

Riding Giants

A powerful analogy to project management is surfing. This may not be immediately obvious... Project managers do not tend to hang out at the beach watching the waves. The Beach Boys also didn't sing much about project management. But in some ways leading a project can feel a lot like surfing. Behind you is a great wave of stakeholder expectations. The wave is made up of everything that is riding on the project – revenue, prestige, reputation for the company and perhaps for the project team also. Ahead is the smooth water where the project delivers and everyone is happy with project success. And in between? There you are, balancing on a small piece of wood. It is a very exposed position and only your individual skills are avoiding the wave crashing down around you.

When considering how the organisation can support project teams, you need to appreciate this stress. As a team takes on bigger projects, with tighter timescales or more limited resource, riding the wave becomes harder. However, there is another way to look at the analogy of the wave. To many project teams, working in isolation from the business, the wave is a threat. It may crash down on them and their project will fail. They can become paralysed by the potential impact to the organisation and even to their own careers. But to the organisation the power of the wave represents the value which the project generates. You want teams to be willing and competent to ride the big waves.

The surfing analogy represents the importance of integrating these two viewpoints. There can be a cultural divide in the organisation between a commercial view, which sees projects (and the wave) as opportunity, and an implementation view, which sees them as a threat. If these are not successfully integrated the project teams may focus too heavily on risk avoidance. Avoiding failure becomes more important than achieving success and teams fail to push to excel.

> *not only were you riding down this mountain but the mountain is chasing after you and you need to figure out how to escape the mountain but also use it.*
>
> *"Riding Giants"*

As a trainer and coach the "surfing" analogy has served me well. I've always been a little nervous using it in California, where I was aware the audience tends to know much more about surf than I do. I was keenly aware that a few of the delegates on my courses in the United States were keen surfers. But the analogy had great value and seemed to work well across cultures. The wave is clearly both a threat and an opportunity. You may tumble and fall off the board but it's also clear that you cannot surf on a flat sea.

Driving out fear

One phrase is critical for successful project culture. The phrase "drive out fear" comes from the work of W.E. Deming. In his work "14 points on Quality Management", Deming proposed key principles for management to follow. These, he said, would build the foundation for significantly improving the effectiveness of an organisation. The concepts which he raised in the "14 points" eventually developed into the ideas of Total Quality Management. These points codified the changes which he felt were needed to build effective organisational culture. His book "Out of the Crisis" was published in 1982 and is still highly respected. Some of the ideas were radical when they were proposed but many of his points would be seen today as key concepts in effective business culture. His eighth rule is especially critical in developing a project culture, and is in many ways perhaps the single most critical cultural concept to implement or promote within project organisations.

> *8. Drive out fear*
>
> *"Out of the Crisis", W.E. Deming*

What does Deming mean by "Drive out fear"? And why do I feel this statement is such a key one for projects? Indeed I would argue it is more critical than the other thirteen, and that perhaps these three words are the key phrase for successful project culture. He is certainly not arguing for blind positivity, which could be hugely destructive to projects. Understanding and managing Risk is a key factor in project success. Ignoring negative signs would not contribute well to any project. Deming is referring to fear as a management technique and to an individual's fear of the consequences of taking action. Effective project culture is centered in openness and communication of issues, unhindered by fear of the response.

 How threatened do teams feel in your organisation? Is the culture one of maximising success or of minimising failure? Do you see people doing the "right" thing or the "safe" thing? How could you make your own team feel more safe?

Many writers have discussed the importance to individuals of security and safety. Perhaps the most famous statement of the importance of these fundamentals is the one below. If security is absent, humans will focus on restoring it in preference to all else.

> *...certain unalienable Rights,*
> *that among these are*
> *Life, Liberty and the pursuit of Happiness.*
>
> **United States Declaration of Independence**

In business terms this idea was developed into the idea of levels of individual desires, made famous by Maslow. Maslow developed the theory known as the "Hierarchy of Needs". This proposes that higher order needs such as self-fulfillment and creativity will flourish only when lower order needs are satisfied.

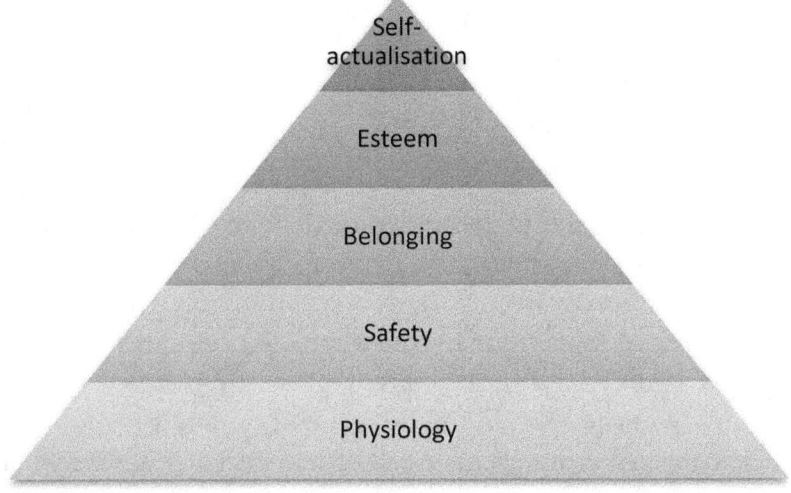

Figure 16 – Maslow's "Hierarchy of Needs"

In a project environment we want teams to deliver value to the business. We need them to be committed and involved. We want them to achieve their full potential. This is partly altruistic but also because this will maximize the benefits that they can supply to the business. In Maslow's terms we need teams to be operating at the top level of his pyramid – Self-actualisation.

But first they need to be safe. We would not expect a team to function effectively without satisfying their physical needs (lighting, heating, technical equipment). Similarly we should not expect them to be effective without the right emotional environment. An environment driven by fear will cause defensive behaviour by the project teams. Their approach to projects will emphasise protecting themselves rather than doing what is best for the project and the organisation.

Symptoms of defensive behaviour

How would you recognise defensive behaviour? Does it matter whether teams are defensive? And what can you do about it? As a leader it is important to understand and manage the behaviours of your teams. Negative behaviours can spread and impact the team ability to deliver. You are not looking to punish the team for the undesired behaviour. That could be counter-productive. It would probably lead to increased protective behaviour by the teams, so promoting the very thing that you are trying to prevent. You are instead trying to assess how you can rebuild the project culture and prevent the negative behaviours from occurring. Left unchecked , defensive behaviour by teams will prevent collaboration and openness and so make projects less effective.

Inflated estimation

Many organisations see issues around estimation. Project estimation sometimes seems to be wildly excessive for the work being undertaken. In some cases, this seems not to be around competence of the team. Indeed you will often observe the more experienced team members to be producing the largest estimates. In some organisations this has reached such a level that realistic planning is heavily impacted. Teams over-estimate wildly and managers then arbitrarily slash the estimates to compensate for the over-estimation, sometimes by as much as half. This behaviour becomes ingrained in the organisation to the degree that it is seen as normal and unavoidable rather than as undesirable.

> To reduce the behaviours and time wasting associated with
> having too much embedded safety, Critical Chain Project
> Management recommends that task estimates are cut to
> half the length of a "normal" duration
>
> **Eli Goldratt**

 What is the typical approach to estimation in your organisation? Do you see most people increasing estimates? Do managers "correct" these estimates? If you find this happens, how do you think it is impacting your organisation?

Let us assume that this is not just an unavoidable behaviour. Instead let us look at why estimate inflation propagates and so how it can be avoided. An organisation may threaten to punish team members who do not deliver every task to their estimate. This is often justified as ensuring that the team work hard. But there will be variance in task duration. In all but the most trivial environment tasks are not wholly predictable. The combination of variance and punishment means that the individual will learn to give an estimate that they can be sure of achieving. If a task will take five days, plus or minus two days, it will be estimated as seven days to ensure that "failure" is avoided. Estimates will move from the most likely to the worst case. Similarly the team lead will want to be sure that the group for which he is responsible delivers within estimate, so he or she will increase the estimates from his team to ensure his personal safety. And the project manager will likewise increase the estimates to ensure he or she isn't at risk for failing to deliver the project.

There may be several levels of management all adding a "safety margin" which aggregates to a vastly inflated project.

The cultural issue here is that the project is driven by fear not by value. An honest planning culture would discuss the estimates, the uncertainties and the confidence level. The organisation would agree a level of margin which gives enough confidence in delivery. This could be used in the most effective way for the project. Most importantly, the organisation would approve the level of risk which is acceptable in the plan rather than leaving the risk to be borne by the individuals. The team can be focused on achieving success in delivering value, not on avoiding failure. This can be by positive measures such as average progress on the project rather than counting "missed estimates".

A team's culture can sometimes be seen in how it responds to new information. If you present a team with data related to its performance, the response can vary hugely. Some teams will want to increase their success, while others will wish to avoid failure. "Increasing success" and "avoiding failure" sound very similar but they drive different behaviours. One is the response of a growing team and one of a defensive team. Many sportsmen have written about the importance of coming to a sporting contest wishing to win, not wishing to avoid losing.

> *"If you don't have confidence, you'll always find a way not to win."*
> *Carl Lewis*

At one point a team that I worked with had an issue with "red" projects. Project managers were asked to maintain a project flag as red, amber or green to indicate their overall confidence level. While most groups would have around 10% of projects "red" at any time, this group had over 40%.
I showed this data to the group management. I had expected to have a discussion around the root cause for the high number and to propose a route forwards. As it happens I didn't believe there was any major issue. I thought it a matter of training the team how the flag was used to ensure more consistency. Instead the management said they would sort out the problem.
And indeed they did. Within two weeks the level of projects in that group which were flagged "red" had dropped to zero and stayed there. Impressive response. A little later I was auditing the group and I asked some of the team what had changed. "Oh, we were told to always mark our projects as green so the group doesn't look bad." was the response.
The group management was frightened of looking bad relative to others. And their lack of confidence meant that rather than trying to improve they focussed on avoiding any perception of failure. It was less risky to conceal the problem than to address it and improve.

Conquering fear

So how do you "drive out fear"? Let's be clear here – this is somewhere that leadership comes from the top. Senior leaders either choose to use fear as a tool or they choose to encourage people to speak up and to try out ideas. More junior roles emulate what they see from the senior roles. Part of the solution is to look closely at the message which you are sending out to the organisation.

> *Tread softly because you tread on my dreams*
>
> *Yeats*

There are some specific areas that can help with this problem. When Deming raised this as a key issue he suggested that a possible solution is to "Encourage effective two-way communication". Certainly, communication seems to be a key factor here. It's no coincidence that the problem of fear as a driver in organisations creeps in with the communication scaling that we discuss in Chapter 3. Small teams with open communication tend to feel less threatened. The structure and nature of small teams leads to openness and a strong support structure.

> *Because we work as a team, we feel supported ...*
> *This gives us the courage to undertake greater challenges.*
>
> ***Scrum values – Scrum Alliance***

Promoting honest and open communication within the organisation will lead to reduced uncertainty within teams. The team will be clear not only what they are doing, but (most critically) why it is important. Changes made to the project, the environment or the team will be visible and understood. The team will find it easier to make decisions because the response to those decisions will be clear and based on visible facts. These factors will reduce the level of fear of unknown threats. And the reduced fear will increase the team's willingness to communicate openly. This builds the "virtuous circle" below.

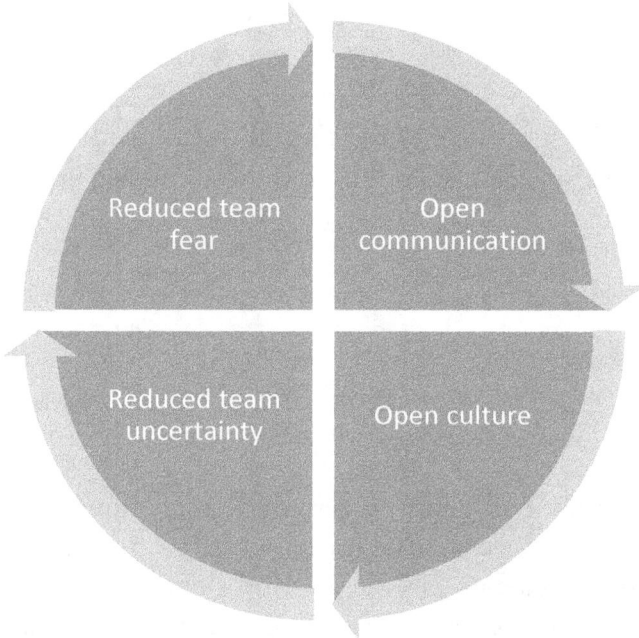

Figure 17 – A "virtuous circle" of driving out fear

Hero Culture

We all like heroes, whether your personal preference is in the mould of Beowulf or Luke Skywalker. From whatever culture you draw your heroes, there's something in human nature that responds to a person with an impossible task, a battle against overwhelming odds and perhaps a final piece of luck that snatches victory from the jaws of defeat. Organisations are no different here. They are typically full of inspirational figures who are presented as "larger than life". These are often founders who struggled in the early days of the company but pulled through to success against huge odds.

> *Nor have I seen a mightier man-at-arms on this earth*
> *than the one standing here*
>
> ***Beowulf***

But let us look again at organisational growth. One dramatic change as the organisation grows is the increased need for the leader to delegate. In the Start-up stage the leader can be highly directive and personally manage all the activities. He or she is typically the expert in the technology and the face of the company. But as the organisation grows, they must delegate to organisational managers, group managers and eventually out to project teams if they achieve a truly collaborative culture. This is not a comfortable experience for all founders.

We can represent the "doing" nature of the leader's role in a growing organisation as below.

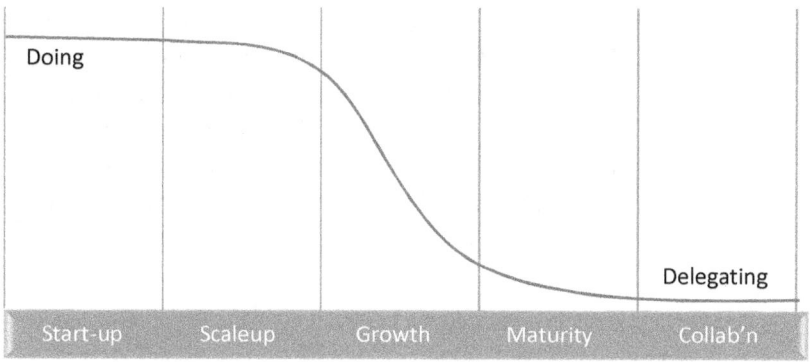

Figure 18 – The leader – doing or delegating?

In the early stages of the organisation, heroes thrive. Unfortunately, the organisation may eventually discover that heroism is not such a good way to operate as you scale. Even worse of course is the possibility that the organisation never does discover this. A "hero culture" implies that key activities are routed through a small number of key individuals. These are usually the managers of the teams. Where does this leave scalability and individual accountability? If it becomes normal and acceptable that an external individual steps in to manage each crisis, then crises can become acceptable to the team. Those external individuals are typically seen as "special" or differently skilled. This means the project team can feel that they are unable themselves to manage a difficult situation. This becomes more embedded as the organisation becomes more established and creates more of its own legends of past events. Today's teams are measured against not against achievable goals but against the exaggerated heroic deeds of a "golden age". Eventually an expectation develops that a hero will appear in any difficulty.

A statement that I recall from one senior manager was "coaching is too slow". He was used to responding to a crisis by instantly stepping in and taking the reins. He would solve the immediate problem and then hand the project back to the team. And he was very good at it. Initially the approach seemed to work well – projects tended to deliver. But as the organisation grew it became visible that this was scaling poorly. The teams had never learned to solve the problems themselves. They expected someone to help them in every crisis, but the "hero" could no longer cover for everyone.

Hero culture can be in direct opposition to project culture. When building an approach to projects you are looking to achieve repeatable delivery. The avoidance of crises is central to your objectives. But hero culture thrives on crisis as it allows the hero to perform. Individuals who have developed in a hero environment can find it hard to adapt to a stable project environment. They may feel they need crises in order to demonstrate their value. They may even generate crises (by delay or distraction) in order to be able to demonstrate their ability.

The idea that teams will artificially create crises sounds extreme. Surely everyone just wants projects that deliver? Who would make them into crises? But I'm sure you know people who delay activities to the last minute? Perhaps you do this yourself? The so-called "student syndrome" (although maybe being a little unfair on students). Like a coffee drinker needing a morning cup, they need to generate a crisis in order to act.

The truly great are daring. They improvise
They do not have protocols and checklists.
Maybe our idea of heroism needs updating.

Atul Gawande, "The Checklist Manifesto"

What does your organisation reward? Are you looking for dramatic heroes or for quiet success? Think about what behaviours you reward and what message this sends to the organisation. Does this promote the behaviours which you want?

When coaching I have often used the phrase "make projects boring". In some ways it's an odd phrase because I don't believe projects are, or ever will be, boring. Certainly not the ones that I have worked on. My point was that you may be operating on the edge of the possible, with huge technical challenges to overcome, and a team and timescales that are stretched. That should be difficulty enough. Why layer on unnecessary difficulties that could be avoided by ensuring that the project approach is straightforward and well understood. Crises are to be minimised, not celebrated.

The phrase "make projects boring" is deliberately controversial. To many people it is even an unattractive prospect – they relish the crises and the chance to use them to shine. But from an organisational viewpoint, I believe "boring" is the objective. Minimise the barriers for the team and this will allow you to attempt projects with more challenging objectives.

Chapter 5

Linking Strategy and Projects

At all stages of an organisation's life we want to gain value from the projects that we run. But how do we do this? How do we ensure that the projects are delivering what we need?

If we want to understand how to make projects deliver value, one solution would be to look only at how projects function. We could focus on building a complex project approach to make them work more efficiently. We could do studies to see where time is lost within the project. It is easy to believe that the major challenge lies in how each individual project is run and that detailed project process is the answer. And how the projects are run is indeed a component of success as we will see later. But projects must be seen as part of the business and how they fit into the business is a key factor to consider first. For the projectised organisation to be effective, it must run smoothly from end to end, not only for individual projects.

Efficiency and Effectiveness

Sometimes well-run projects still don't deliver what the business needs. Although outwardly the project seems to be working well, and it delivers outputs at the right time, it is not generating value for the organisation. If we are to make projects effective in the organisation we will need to resolve this. To explore this problem, we need to distinguish two different, but related concepts - Efficiency and Effectiveness. Although these very similar words are often used interchangeably, there is an important distinction between them. A careful distinction has been built in the Quality Management discipline, as summed up by the quote below.

> *Efficiency is doing the thing right.*
> *Effectiveness is doing the right thing.*
>
> *Peter F. Drucker*

Efficiency is about the way a project executes. A parallel can be drawn with the definition of Efficiency in Physics. In this case Efficiency is the useful work output divided by the energy input. We can similarly define project efficiency as below. Of course, measuring this can be more of a challenge than stating it.

> *Efficiency: The ratio of the useful work performed in a process to the total effort expended*

Much of the discipline of project management is focused on project efficiency. A project is planned, monitored and controlled to ensure that the expected work is undertaken by the right people at the right time. Possible delays are anticipated and managed. Scope is managed to ensure that effort is optimally targeted. This is intended to maximize the chance of successful delivery of the expected outputs. Efficiency is very much a focus of the "project" view of the world.

Effectiveness by contrast is about how well those outputs align to organisational goals. This is much closer to the "strategic" viewpoint and addresses the value of the project to the business. A project could be run efficiently but still not be effective in generating a value for the business. It could be that the "wrong" work is being performed, even though efficiently.

> *Effectiveness: The degree to which something is successful in producing a desired result*

 Think about the people who run projects in your organisation. Do they strive for efficiency or effectiveness? Are they measured by delivery of what was asked for or what the organisation really needs?

Efficiency and Effectiveness are not opposites. It is perfectly possible to create effective projects and to run them efficiently.

But these is often a tension between the two, as there often is between the "project" and the "strategy" viewpoint. A good analogy is archery. Efficiency is about how you draw the bow, the power of the shot and the skill of aiming. But Effectiveness is about choosing the right target. It is very easy to focus "improvement" only on the "how" part of increased Efficiency and to fail to integrate this into what the organisation needs.

Effectiveness requires the organisation to drive the projects. This sounds obvious but an organisation could easily end up driven bottom-up by its projects. This can lead to significant problems. This situation arises when projects are created "ad hoc" around the organisation without an overall approach. Perhaps the projects are solving local problems, or they are implementing promising technical capabilities. Perhaps projects are started because they are possible, not because they are needed. If these fail to tie in well with strategy, it risks increasing efficiency without increasing value to the business. The organisation may respond to the lack of increased value by trying to push to increase efficiency further. This can lead to a spiral of increasing process as organisations try to do more to make the projects "perform".

Organisational alignment

While efficiency can be improved by project process, effectiveness is improved by aligning the projects with the organisation. Unless the organisation is already well structured and running smoothly, this can be an area where major gains can often be made. But to make these gains you may have to step back from the detail and look at the bigger picture.

> *There is nothing quite so useless as doing with great efficiency something that should not be done at all.*
>
> *Peter F. Drucker*

We must not focus on the projects in isolation. We need to look at the way that the organisational need is determined, how this generates projects and how the projects deliver value back into the organisation. This needs to be seen as a joined-up process, rather than considering the intent – the strategy – separately from the implementation – the projects.

> *However beautiful the strategy,*
> *you should occasionally look at the results.*
>
> *Winston Churchill*

One of the groups that I worked with saw a huge reduction in cost overruns. When I started with the group it had average overruns of 100%. Yes, that's right – on <u>average</u> each project spent double the predicted cost. This cost was almost entirely cost of internal effort, which meant the projects were taking double the approved work. Of course, this didn't only hit the "bottom line" of the organisation, it also had a huge opportunity cost, leading to large resourcing repercussions.

Within two years this overrun had dropped to 10%. When I quote this change people usually ask what project processes I put in to make the changes.   In other words, what was the efficiency change? But this wasn't really due to project efficiency gains.

What I did was bring together the developers, project managers, marketing and management to look at the way they worked together to define and approve projects. The 100% overrun didn't indicate poor project efficiency, it indicated poor business effectiveness. The products weren't always well defined and the approved budgets were often unrealistic.

"Hold on!" you may say, "Did you halve the project cost or not?". Well, the project costs didn't halve. But the overruns did reduce that much. The main change was that by working together the organisation produced plans and budgets which were more realistic than the old budgets. And yes, that meant they were higher. The effectiveness increase came from having an end-to-end joined up organisation. This led to less requirements churn and less resource churn. The right products were being made more predictably.

As with any interface, there are challenges involved. Interfacing between strategy and projects is important but is not easy and involves some challenges. The organisational level tends to have high uncertainty and low detail, while the project level is the opposite. This means that there will probably be individuals with different styles and skills operating in these two areas. Strategic planners do not necessarily want, value or manage well the level of detail present in projects. Project managers are not necessarily comfortable with the level of uncertainties involved in strategic planning. Communication between the two therefore may be challenging.

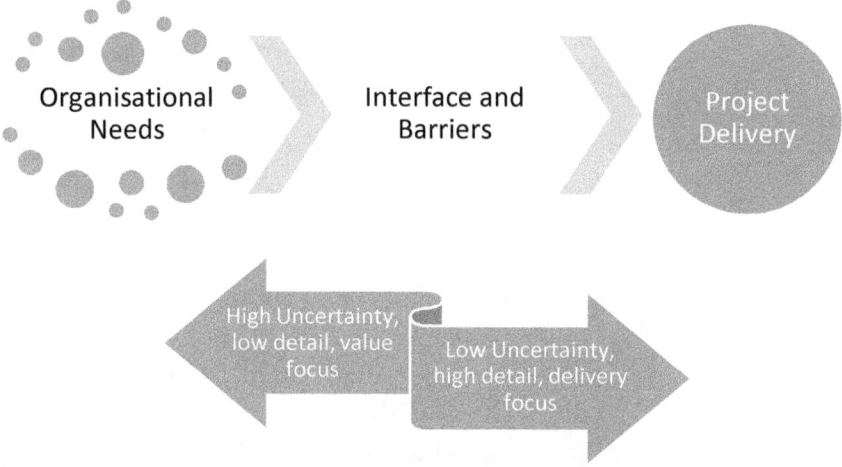

Figure 19- Organisational need to project delivery

Using P3M as an interface

There is value in having a clearly defined interface between strategy and implementation. There are a range of hierarchical approaches in use, but no uniform accepted definition of the layers involved. Typical levels here are named Portfolios, Program(me)s and Projects, but interpretation of these can vary widely. One model for this interface is P3M (an abbreviation for "Portfolio, Programme and Project Management"). The descriptions here are based on the "P3M3" maturity model which was developed by the UK's Office of Government Commerce (OGC).

Figure 20- The P3M model

The terminology here is far from standardized. Looking at advertised job roles, you will see "Portfolio Project Managers" or "Project/Program Managers", used as if the terms were largely equivalent. You will see differences in spelling ("Program" or "Programme") adding to the confusion. Let's look at the layers as they are used in the P3M model, what they mean and how they can be used to join the organisation to the teams doing the work.

The model can be summarized fairly simply. We will go into more detail about each of the layers later. Looking at the diagram overleaf, at one end we have the organisational strategy. At the other we have the teams executing tasks. The diagram is horizontal as I prefer to view this as a horizontal pipeline, rather than a vertical "management on top" hierarchy. A pipeline gives a clearer representation of transferring information and transitioning between organisational need and project delivery.

Drawn horizontally, the diagram can be read left to right. Each layer delivers something critical to the layers to the right and receives something in return. So for example, a Portfolio is focused on defining the value that the organisation needs to receive from an activity. It typically does this through defining a business case. This looks at what is needed for the organisational value, the constraints and what level of resources could be justified. This is passed to the Programme and becomes a key tool for that layer. The Programme uses the business case for guidance about what outcomes are needed, the available budgets, the constraints and risk appetite.

The layered approach allows a structured transition from the organisational need to the project delivery. Each layer is a balance of complexity, uncertainty and detail. The owner of the layer maintains oversight over the layers on the right, ensuring that the correct value is delivered. Each layer delivers outputs to the layers on the left, satisfying the value and using the more detailed knowledge to report on progress and ensure delivery.

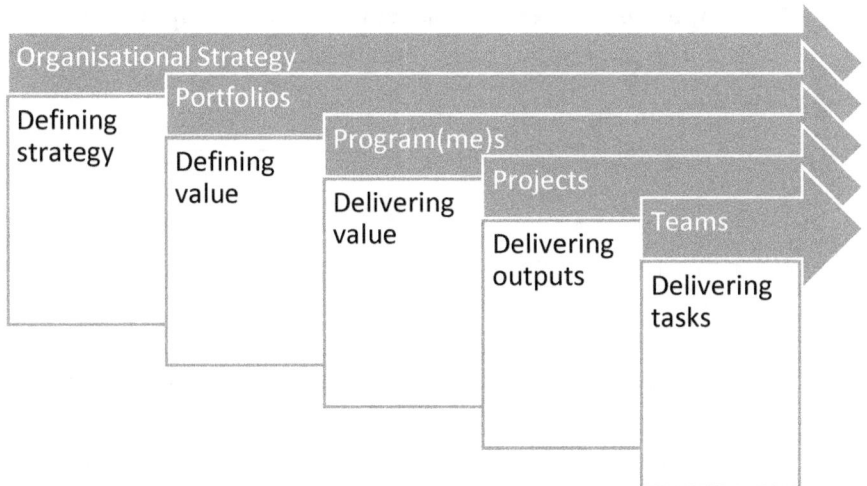

Figure 21- P3M – strategy to tasks

Chapter 6

Portfolios

Let's look at the first "P" – "Portfolio". While the term "project" is widely used, "portfolio" may be less familiar to readers and is certainly less standardised in meaning. In general English usage, the term can mean any collection. For example it can often be used to describe a collection of investments. Originally the name just comes from a set of sheets of paper stored together, where the papers have any meaning.

> *Portfolio: A range of products or services offered by an organisation*
>
> *Oxford English Dictionary*

But in the context of organisations we mean something more specific. A "portfolio" in the P3M context is the set of organisational activities. Some of these the organisation is currently working on or planning to do. These are included in the portfolio because they represent plans and commitments.

The portfolio also contains items which are not definite but which it may do, depending on capacity. These are items which can demonstrate a return but may not be the most rewarding for the organisation. And we must also consider those that the organisation could do but chooses not to do. An understanding of possibilities which are not currently planned (and why) also needs to be considered and managed within the overall portfolio.

> *The focus of portfolio management is ...*
> *the organisation's strategy*
>
> **Portfolio, Programme and Project Offices - Axelos**

A portfolio can be split into three main areas or categories of work:

•Business as Usual (BAU).   •This is the ongoing activity of the business.

☐It may be part of the effective running of the business (for example the on-going activities of a Finance department).

☐Alternatively it may directly generate revenue (for example the operational activities of manufacturing or distribution).

•Improvement Programmes.   •These are activities intended to improve the BAU part of the business.

☐These are change programmes which may involve reducing cost, increasing efficiency or quality.

☐The outcome is that the business as a whole is more effective.

•Development Programmes.   •These are programmes which will directly develop new products or services.

☐Once complete these can be moved into the BAU part of the business to be managed, sold and supported.

Pipeline Management

The portfolio decides how to invest in the three areas. The "pipeline" is the sequence of forthcoming programmes. Pipeline Management is about planning and scheduling investment in the Development and Improvement Programme types. In any organisation there are always immediate needs, possibly even current crises. But an exclusive focus on today's crises risks starving the future programmes which might alleviate those very crises. Pipeline Management therefore is the balancing of immediate need against change to ensure that the organisation delivers today and grows for what is needed tomorrow.

Neither side of the balance may be allowed to dominate. An organisation which prioritises today's crises will find itself unable to grow and improve. While an organisation which prioritises improvement projects risks being unable to sustain its business and cash flow. You need to maintain a sound enough base to be able to fund the development and implement strategy.

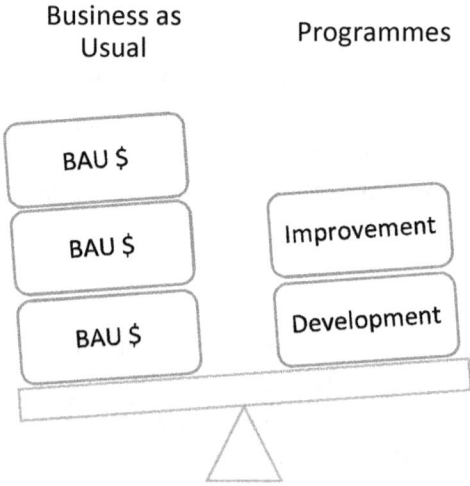

Figure 22- Pipeline Management – a balancing act

Resources are scarce. It is a rare (or unimaginative) organisation that can even attempt everything which it can imagine.   Any organisation will find that it must make decisions about what to target. If you attempt too many activities, your investment in each will necessarily be reduced and your chance of success of any will be lowered. The analogy is often used of a funnel where the wide end is the space of possible actions and the narrow end is the available resources for action.

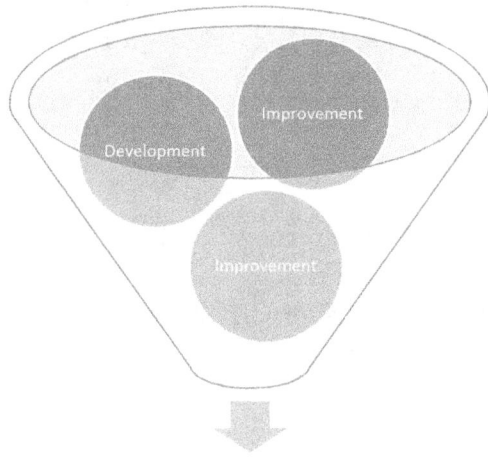

New Programme

Figure 23- Pipeline of activities

Portfolio management therefore is the formalisation of deciding which activities will be attempted. It is not about the execution of these activities, and does not guarantee that they will succeed. It does however define the activities and the expected benefits to be gained by undertaking them. By formalising the decision-making process, portfolio management ensures that the correct activities are chosen.

Research has shown that portfolio management is a way to bridge the gap between strategy and implementation

Project Management Institute

Portfolio Decision Making

The approach used for choosing activities will vary. In general however a portfolio is balancing risk and reward. The objective is to choose the activities with the best return for the business. This should judge against the following criteria:

- There is no alternative activity with higher value and the same level of risk
- There is no alternative activity with the same value and lower risk.

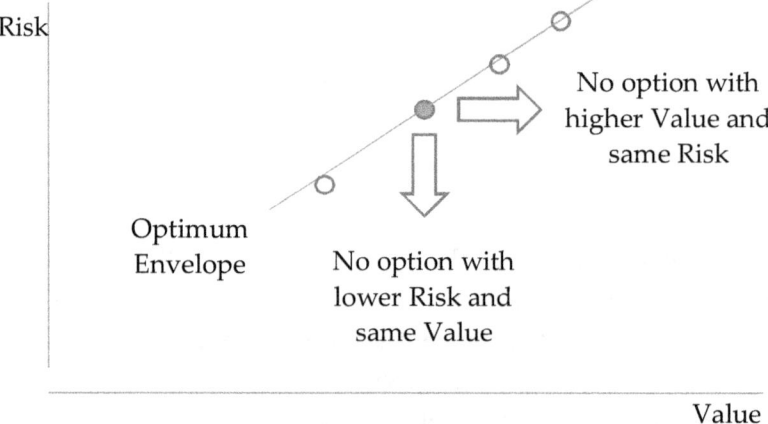

Figure 24- Optimising the portfolio

This can be a challenge to assess, especially when trading off an immediate crisis against a long-term benefit. Studies have shown that the perception of risk is strongly affected by proximity in time and space. The risk level of immediate events is perceived as much higher than the risk of equivalent, but far-off events. A good evolutionary trait perhaps - when faced with a sabre-toothed tiger, you stop worrying about the harvest. However it may be less optimal when planning a strategy. The portfolio therefore needs realistically to trade off not only benefits, but also risks.

Portfolio management is especially challenging because it is the "art of the possible". There is never enough resource to achieve every desired programme. To succeed, not only must the programmes be realistically prioritised, but the capacity must be realistically estimated. Portfolio modelling refers to the alignment of capability with priorities. Each scenario of programmes has a specific resourcing need, both in number and skills. Optimising the scenario typically involves more than just selecting the top rated programmes up to the level of resource capacity because of key factors, some of which are below:

Programme RoI

A programme might be rated as number one for importance but may not be the best choice. This may sound contradictory but the key factor is that its resource needs may be high. By dropping that programme, it might be possible to resource both the second and third programmes instead. This could lead to a greater overall return if the value of all of the top programmes is similar. It will be important to consider not only the absolute value of programmes but also the cost and so the return on investment.

Programme skills

Individuals are not identically skilled. As a result, a programme which has high demands on a specific skill set may effectively block a large number of other programmes. Portfolio planning therefore needs to balance "Opportunity cost". It must consider not only the benefits from a specific programme, but the loss of opportunity in other programmes which cannot be undertaken as a result. Critical skills could be the defining factor in the portfolio, reducing the capability of the organisation below its potential.

Portfolio planning is often managed by tracking numbers of people. As a starting point this is a valuable approach. But people are not equivalent. This can lead to an over-estimate of capability, because there are often the right <u>number</u> of people but not the right <u>mix</u> of people.

I've seen environments where one critical resource type defines the whole programme. For example, there may be a limited number of people with the skills (technical and personal) to lead a project. If you have only four project leaders, you can run only four parallel projects.

Increasing capability

Organisational capability is not static. As discussed above, some limits of skill or capability may constrain a portfolio's overall value. The solution must be considered over long timeframes, and the portfolio must be built not only on today's capabilities but on the anticipated capability in the future. Indeed the portfolio must not just respond to, but actively drive, increasing capability by targeted hiring and investing in training and coaching, rather than just prioritising based on current available capability.

Important or urgent?

One key factor in building an effective portfolio is the difference between importance and urgency. An important programme is one which will make a big difference to the organisation. It might bring a high financial return. It might be critical for governance of the organisation, potentially introducing major risk if not performed. Or it may have a huge impact on the performance of the organisation as a whole. An urgent programme is one which has a very short timeframe. If done at all it must be started now or very soon, and it must be progressed very quickly.

> *What is important is seldom urgent*
> *and what is urgent is seldom important.*
>
> *Dwight Eisenhower*

Although urgency and importance are often seen as identical, they are largely independent parameters. Urgency relates to the timeframe of the programme and importance relates to the value to the organisation. There is a common human tendency to focus time and effort on urgent programmes. These will give visible returns in a very short time. An important but non-urgent programme may take a longer period to show any visible results. People often feel more positive about being part of urgent programmes. In an organisation which prioritises rapid and visible results, staff may actually be disproportionately rewarded for these activities.

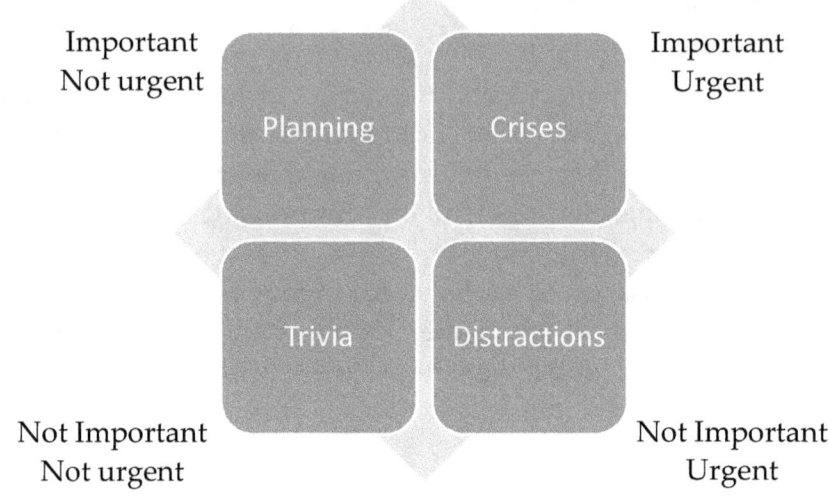

Important
Not urgent

Important
Urgent

Planning

Crises

Trivia

Distractions

Not Important
Not urgent

Not Important
Urgent

Figure 25- Importance and urgency

Balancing the roadmap

"Balancing" is the step which transforms a roadmap from an interesting set of aspirations to a valuable tool. A "balanced roadmap" is one which has been demonstrated to be realistic and achievable for the organisation. This allows it to move from being a "wish list" of what the organisation might desire to being an achievable plan which drives the organisation forwards.

To achieve a balanced roadmap you need to undertake some level of planning for each programme. As with any planning, you are looking at the resources which are required and the dependencies or alignment with other work. This can be quite challenging to achieve. Knowledge may be spread around the organisation and so this initial planning may involve many people from different parts. Historic data is needed to assess on-going activities or the real size of past projects. Uncertainty levels may be high and people may be unwilling to produce initial estimates for fear that they may be constrained by these at a later point. It may also be a challenge to predict what the organisation's capability to deliver will be. In a strongly growing organisation, it may be hard to assess what teams, of what skills, will be available at a specific date.

It is important to understand that the balanced roadmap is not a project plan. Perhaps the roadmap includes a new product next year which has been estimated to take ten people for six months. This does not mean that the end date of the eventual project is committed. What is *does* mean is that the organisation has made a sincere effort to allocate enough space to give that project a good chance of success. An appropriate level of resource will be made available, and delivery expectations will be realistic.

Balancing a roadmap is a challenging exercise. Managing all of the associated data is difficult. The biggest challenge isn't in the process, but in keeping the planning process "honest". There is generally a huge desire to have roadmap items earlier to satisfy customer demand. As a result it is tempting to make an unrealistic roadmap, built on optimistic assumption and underestimates. Unfortunately this helps no-one. Unsurprisingly the projects "fail" to deliver on the roadmap which is not achieved. The over-ambitious roadmap leads to over-commitment, crisis management and resources pulled from one project to another. Quality and customer experience suffer, project teams feel they are failing and what is achieved is generally less successful than would have come from a more realistic roadmap.

A realistic roadmap is a key factor in effective project delivery. Groups that say "Projects are always delivering late" often really mean "We are telling our customers roadmap dates which we cannot achieve".

One group that I worked with would generate a roadmap each year which would need about 20% more people than they had available. The management knew that the roadmap was unrealistic. So why did they do this? They didn't want to have a difficult conversation with customers to say that they would not be making some products.

As I say in "Value driven Project Planning", realistic planning inevitably causes conflict. This is just as true at this level as at the project level.

The day-to-day reality of project delivery in that group was pretty grim. Constant crises led to constant movement of people between projects. Most teams expected to end a project blamed for late delivery and as a result few were motivated to try and deliver to a roadmap that they knew was unachievable.

Chapter 7

Projects

What is a project?

What is a meal? An easy question? There are clearly components involved and common features between meals. But your culture and experience shapes your expectations of what will be delivered, how it will be prepared and how it will arrive

In the same way most people feel that they know what a "project" is. But having a common understanding can be a challenge. There will be different views across organisations which are implementing project management.

Just as you want to know what you will be eating when you order in a restaurant, so you need to establish a common understanding on what a project actually is in your organisation.

Let's try and agree on the meaning of "project". Surely that is straightforward? Well, there's a good test for this. If you ask people what they think is a project (and I've done this many times when training) what do they say? The most common responses see a project as integrating a goal with a degree of planning or management. Perhaps they say there is a team or a budget. Or they talk about tasks, milestones and risks. But which of these really define a project as a project?

Let's start with a dictionary definition or "project". This perhaps represents the widely-understood meaning of the term.

> *Project: An individual or collaborative enterprise that is carefully planned to achieve a particular aim*
>
> ***Oxford English Dictionary***

This definition however has some limitations. Is an activity only a project if "carefully planned"? And if so, how carefully? Haven't we all seen badly planned projects – do they cease to be projects? If we leap in and start immediately with no planning at all, is it therefore no longer a project? And if not, what is it? What about Business as Usual activities? The organisational payroll has clear planning and reliably achieves defined aims – is it a project? These questions may sound trivial, but surely a clear definition of projects must be critical to development of a projectised organisation.

When looking at new groups or acquisitions, agreeing on projects was usually the starting point. We needed to have a common understanding of what a "project" was and what projects we were undertaking.

In one example, all current on-going work for the group was being added into "the project". This would be a mixture of planned work (such as feature development), reactive work (such as bug fixing) and Business as Usual (such as customer support). After some workshops we agreed how to partition this work into a small number of distinct projects and ensured that everyone understood where the boundaries lay.

In another team, every piece of work was a project. It might only be a few days for one individual, but it was carefully set up, assigned a project manager, planned and documented. Here the team needed to realise that these were work packages or tasks and could be grouped into larger projects which could more effectively be managed and reported. With hundreds of tiny projects the true picture was being lost.

We need an understanding which is clearly targeted to the project environment. Let us look at a definition of a project from a leading project management organisation. How does this view projects?

> *Project: a temporary endeavor undertaken to create a unique product or service*
>
> ***Project Management Institute***

There are two key features in this definition. Firstly there is the temporary nature of the undertaking, which has a start and an end. The project is time-bounded rather than continuous. The second key feature is the generation of a change. There is something at the end of the project which was not there at the beginning. This may be a physical object, a deliverable of some sort, or a change in approach due to the project.

This gives us some helpful guidelines. If a project generates change then our "Business As Usual" work is excluded. Managing the payroll or manufacturing clearly defined products are not projects. They are repeatable activities. Their intent is to leave the business unchanged at the end.

The "temporary" concept has undergone some evolution over the years. A few years ago, it was clear that a team came together, delivered their project and then went on their ways. The project had a clear start and an end. But with more diverse projects, especially the introduction of Agile approaches, this is now less accepted. Software projects may work with a fixed team on one code base for years. Time is still an important dimension. Each individual change is implemented in a phase (or timebox or however the approach refers to this). But the lifetime of the project itself may be less clear. Change is continual over a long time span.

Outputs not value

A project delivers a "unique product or service". We know when it will run and what it will produce (at least over some planned horizon). By using this definition we are able to control the project. This lets us break down the work, sequence activities, work out how to use the team most effectively and how to minimise risk.

All of these make it more straightforward for those on the project team to deliver. There will of course be challenges in execution, which might include technical complexity, stakeholder agreement, compliance risk or many other areas, but the project gives a framework. Many techniques have been developed to deliver projects effectively and these are grounded in the fact that projects are focused on delivery of specific outputs. Since we know what we are trying to achieve, we can optimise how we will achieve it.

This is both the strength and the weakness of projects. By focussing on outputs the project ensures delivery. Uncertainty is reduced to allow the team to focus on making the outputs. But by focussing on outputs you necessarily reduce the focus on value. The need to deliver forces the separation between the project delivery world view and the strategic portfolio world view.

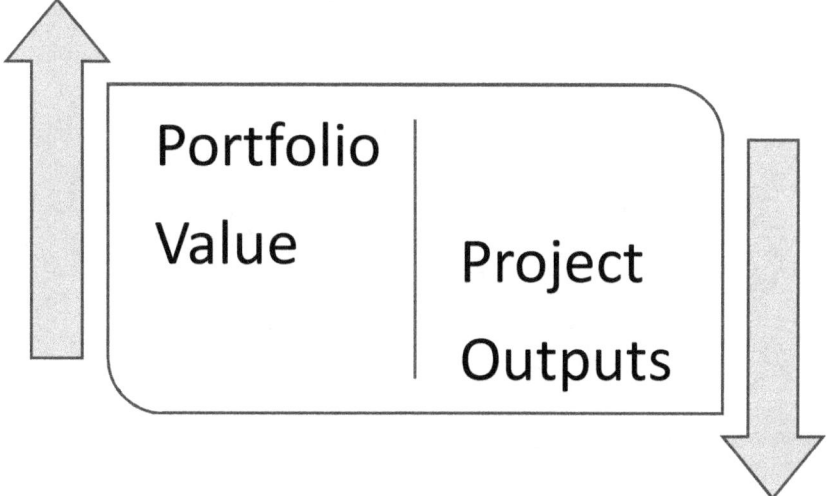

Figure 26- Focussing on outputs or on value

Engineering organisations can become over-focused on technology. I've worked with teams that would ensure that projects had a clear focus on ensuring that the technology became deliverables for customers. By creating a project, we could ensure momentum towards delivering the outputs and so generating value for customers and the organisation.

The challenge is to make sure that what you strive to create is what the customers want. To do that you need to be effective at joining the strategy to the execution.

I worked with one team that were very talented and hard working. They decided on one project they were going to do the very best that they could. They made a product that was not just what they were asked to make but outperformed the targets by about 20%. At the end of the project they were understandably delighted, and a little stunned, by what they had done. Viewed as outputs, they had created some impressive technology.

But viewed as business value, the position was different. In their focus on delivery they had become wholly disconnected from the strategy. The portfolio had wanted a product to fit on a long-term roadmap. What the team had made had destroyed that roadmap as there would be no "improved" product next year. Effectively a year's potential value had been given away with a great output, but a poor outcome.

Chapter 8

Programmes

What joins projects and portfolios? If the project is execution focused and tightly constrained, and the portfolio is strategy based and more open-ended, we will need something in the middle. Otherwise projects and portfolios will not speak the same language. We risk improving projects until we have great execution and improving portfolios until we have great strategy but still be unable to join the two. Effectiveness, not efficiency alone, is again the goal.

This connection is the role of the "Programme". This is not a term with a well-standardised meaning. A dictionary might define a programme as below:

> *Programme: A planned series of future events*
>
> ***Oxford English Dictionary***

Common usage is again too generic for our needs. This definition could just as easily apply to a project.

You may spot a recurring theme here. Many project and programme management terms seem to be poorly defined. This lack of common understanding is part of what seems to make it hard to agree a project approach. Shared language is often a key focus need for building project capability. And shared language can be harder to achieve than you might expect.

Recently I saw a project team criticised for missing a plan date of "January 17th". No, they explained, they had been presenting "January 17" meaning "January 2017" not "January 17th". And how often have we seen project reports confused whether "3/4" means the third of April or the fourth of March?

The Project Management Institute (PMI) offer a 15 page "Lexicon of Project Management terms", summarised in the figure below. It's pretty daunting. It's no real exaggeration to say that each team needs to establish its terms at a project or organisational level before it gets started, just as much as if they spoke different languages. My "Business Case" is your "Project Definition Document" or my "Sprint Review" is your "Project Meeting".

Why is this the case? Well perhaps it is because projects evolved in different places. It's hard to stretch the same terms from the root of projects in construction or in aerospace to the range of current usage. But also often the separate language seems to be used to create mystique. Abbreviations and acronyms abound, usually without explanation. This leads to a set of "qualified" initiates. And to all the opportunities for training and making money from teaching.

Figure 27- Project language (after PMI Lexicon)

So what is a Programme and how is it distinct from a Project, at least within the P3M model?. A Programme is the layer that takes the business need from the Portfolio and generates the Projects to solve that need. We can see it defined for the P3M model below.

> *Programme – A temporary flexible organization structure created to coordinate, direct and oversee the implementation of a set of related projects and activities in order to deliver outcomes and benefits related to an organization's strategic objectives*
>
> ***Managing Successful Programmes***

The Programme avoids the constraints on a project. Where a project is time-bounded, a programme is potentially open ended. Where a project delivers outputs, a programme delivers value ("outcomes and benefits" in the definition above). More generally a programme is responsible for translating the open-ended, value based view of a portfolio into the bounded, output-based view of a set of projects.

A change programme is hard to model as a project. Why is there a difficulty here? The change will typically include some feedback as it develops. Since it responds to its environment, it will be impossible fully to specify at the start. The nature of the programme may mean that multiple stages prove to be required. The change may evolve with a stage being executed as a project, the results retrieved and assessed and a new stage planned and executed as a new project based on the initial results.

A development programme may also be more complex than a single project. The programme may produce one or more products which go through a complex lifecycle of development, release, support, extension, modification, maintenance and eventual retirement. The lifecycle will depend on external factors which are not predictive. Multiple projects may be needed to address the full lifecycle. The diagram below shows a typical lifecycle of a product and how it might be modelled as a programme of different projects.

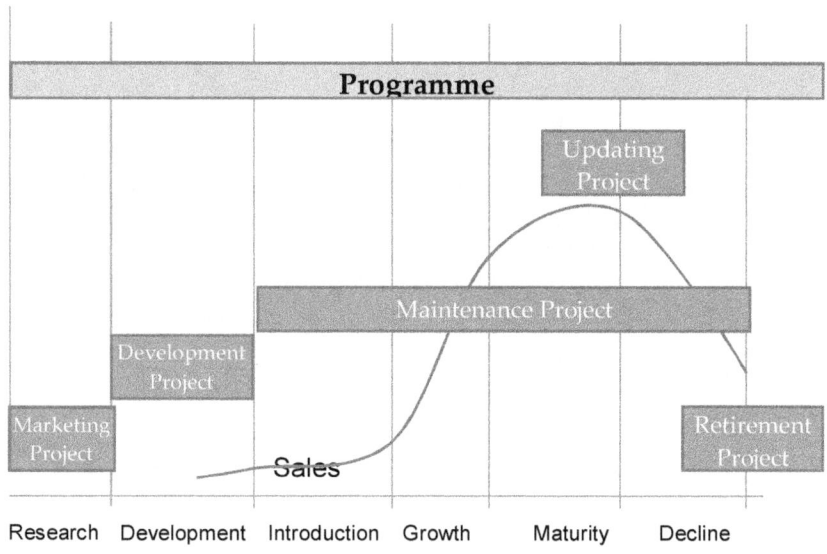

Figure 28 – Product life cycle and programme

Program or Programme?

You will see "Programme" spelt with or without a trailing "-me". The difference in spelling is regional, with "Programme" used more in the UK and "Program" in the US. It is worth being aware of the slight usage differences as the two terms are not quite equivalent. Compare these definitions.

The first is from the US.

> *Program - A group of related projects managed in a coordinated way to obtain benefits and control not available from managing them individually*
>
> ***Project Management Institute (US)***

The second we have already met and comes from the UK.

> *Programme – A temporary flexible organization structure created to coordinate, direct and oversee the implementation of a set of related projects and activities in order to deliver outcomes and benefits related to an organization's strategic objectives*
>
> ***Managing Successful Programmes (UK)***

The difference between the two definitions is significant. Both the US and UK variants are discussing a layer between projects and portfolios.

The US definition of "program" is described as rolling upwards. It is defined in terms of co-ordinating related projects. The projects have an existing identity of their own and "Program Management" is then a layer added on top to improve the management of the projects.

The UK definition is subtly different. A "programme" concept pushes downwards, implementing strategy through creating projects. The projects exist because the programme needs them in order to reach its goals. "Programme Management", rather than co-ordinating projects, generates them to deliver strategy.

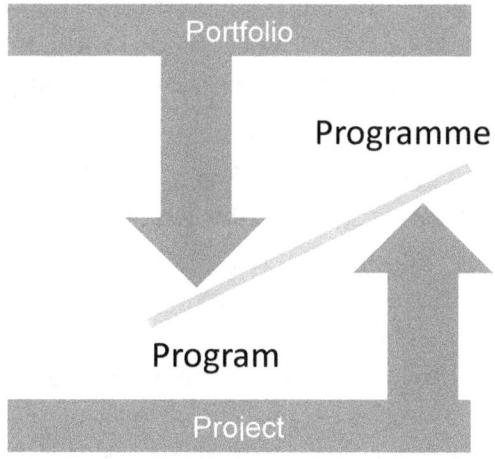

Figure 29 – Program and Programme concepts

We are endeavouring to link strategy to implementation. It is important to remember therefore that alignment between projects is not enough. The purpose of the Programme layer is to ensure that value is delivered back to the Portfolio.

Isn't this all rather complex?

I suspect at this point you are feeling this is more detailed than it need be. The description above is a layered model that can be used in a fully evolved organisation. Perhaps you are at an early stage of the organisational lifecycle with a smaller and simpler organisation. Or maybe you are just feeling this is overly complex and maybe a bit formal. Three layers with clearly separated responsibility? This seems a little excessive if you currently have one product and one or two customers. You know the customers well. Maybe you feel the need for project management to increase repeatable delivery but not the need for the full P3M model. And surely I don't mean that you need three people (Portfolio, Programme and Project managers) just to organise a project?

The good news is that I'm not suggesting everyone adopt a complex framework. I see P3M as a valuable conceptual model that describes three sets of activities which are critical to the project organisation. The partitioning used in the model helps in understanding the factors that need to be managed somewhere in the organisation. The amount of effort in each of the three areas will depend on the size and structure of the organisation. Initially the focus is likely to be on individual projects and how they are managed. This formalisation at the project level will be about increasing repeatability and predictability of delivery. As the organisation grows you may find that you need to manage beyond individual projects. You will be developing follow-on projects and related projects. Products will start to evolve through their lifecycle. Fairly rapidly there will be families of related projects. This will lead to Programme management, possibly close on the tail of Project management.

Up to this point the market drivers for Programmes may have been obvious. But eventually you may find that the market complexity has grown. A more rigorous approach to portfolios is needed. Running projects efficiently is still needed but efficiency is being overtaken by effectiveness as the key issue. Every project remains a delivery challenge, although the approach may now be well understood. However choosing and targeting the projects becomes just as great a challenge. This builds the Portfolio element as in the diagram below.

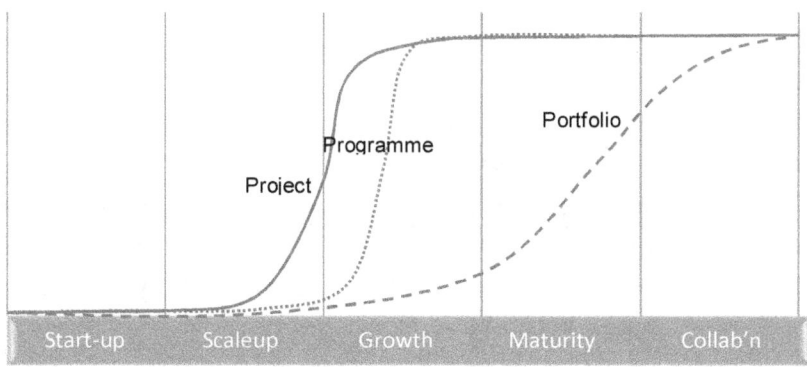

Figure 30 – The growth of the P3M layers

Organisations can simplify the model. One simplification would be to drop Programmes entirely. If the organisation is small, the Portfolio is generating widely-understood activities. These can be directly managed as Projects with clearly defined outputs and scope. There remains a risk of separation between strategy and implementation, but this is manageable in a small organisation.

Another alternative is to combine Programmes and Projects. This is closer to the typical Agile approaches. An Agile project maintains a Programme-like flexibility by proceeding in staged iterations and by keeping a high level of customer feedback to maximise value. But it does this at a Project scale – instead of creating projects it creates iterations or timeboxes as short, fixed scope implementations.

Chapter 9

Building the new world

You understand where you want to get to. Your organisation is growing and you can get value from more formal project approaches. Perhaps the organisation is in a Scaleup stage trying to move beyond fighting fires. Maybe you are in a Growth stage wanting a structure to support the expanding business. Or maybe you have reached the Maturity stage with frightening speed and realise that the controls and structure were left behind in the rush.

How hard is it to implement the transition that you want to achieve? Well, there are going to be some challenges. The good news is that the basics are far from impossible, but you should accept that the practicalities of making it work can be challenging.

PMOs

You need a mechanism to deliver a formalised approach into the company. And you also need a way to manage that change. The mechanism used is often referred to as a "PMO". The problem with talking about "PMO"s is that there is little common understanding about PMOs. Indeed, even what the term "PMO" stands for is somewhat disputed. The "P" is variously interpreted as "Project" or "Program" (or regionally "Programme") or "Portfolio". Or all three at once. A typical definition of "PMO" is below. I've reproduced this at some length just to show how wide ranging the uncertainties around PMOs can be. This quote comes from a world-leading project management organisation trying to explain a PMO.

> *A project management office (PMO) is an organizational body or entity assigned various responsibilities related to the centralized and coordinated management of those projects under its domain.*
> *The responsibilities of a PMO can range from providing project management support functions to responsibility for the direct management of a project.*
> *The projects supported or administered by the PMO may not be related other than by being managed together.*
> *The specific form, function, and structure of a PMO are dependent on the needs of the organization that it supports. A PMO may be delegated the authority to act as an integral stakeholder and a key decision maker during the beginning of each project, to make recommendations, or to terminate projects or take other actions as required to keep business objectives consistent.*
> *In addition, the PMO may be involved in the selection, management, and deployment of shared or dedicated project resources*
>
> **A Guide to the Project Management Body of Knowledge**
> **Project Management Institute (2008)**

This quote shows the broadness of interpretation. The definition is so wide and all-encompassing it has little meaning and probably less value to a user. Every sentence seems to be qualified by "may" or "can". Different organisations with different needs have used the name "PMO" to fit their own requirements, and any attempt to define the PMO has been fitted on at a later date. So when I say creating a "PMO" to implement and manage a change towards improved project approaches, I'm going to need to define what I mean a little more clearly.

Confusion in language is a common theme in this book. Don't underestimate how much of a barrier the lack of common understanding of the "PMO" name can be. Because the role of the PMO is not well known, suspicion and mistrust can easily creep in. The parody of the "process improvement person" with a manual and a stick to beat people into submission is a widely-shared meme. It is important to be clear what the PMO means. This includes why it offers value to the organisation and also why it offers value to the practitioners themselves. Unless these two messages are clear, by default many people will view the PMO at best as an irrelevance and at worst as a threat.

We can use the P3M model to put some more structure on to what this group might be and what it might achieve. Remember that P3M includes Projects, Programmes and Portfolios. P3M uses the term "P3O" for "Project, Programme and Portfolio Office". The full name is a bit unwieldy, but it makes it clear that the potential scope is across **all** of the layers of the model. So in this book we will avoid the fairly overused and ambiguous "PMO" term in favour of "P3O". Of course this hasn't directly solved the problem. The scope of a P3O is even larger than a PMO and is described more generically in the P3M model.

> *P3O: The decision-enabling and support business model for*
> *all business change within an organisation.*
>
> *Portfolio, Programme and Project Offices: Axelos*

This definition refers to business change but could equally refer to product delivery or any other project based activity. Whatever the goals of the organisation, if this is being achieved through projects, the projects will need some support. The support can be through structures built within each project and disbanded at the end of the project. However, where a wider organisational structure is used then this is a form of P3O.

Working in this area with one group we adopted the older name "PMO" for "Project Management Office". Although "PMO" is more recognised, I prefer "P3O" as an overall term. As you can see, there's a lot of potential scope that a P3O can cover, and using the "PMO" name tends to imply you are only going to look at a small part of this.

I found that referring to a "P3O" implied an open cross-organisational scope. This promoted discussion about how the new P3O would work with the organisation. However, using the name "PMO" tended to be viewed as a closed scope. The general understanding was of detailed process and focussing on supporting project managers.   This would shut down conversation with many stakeholders.

Again, the language used is critical and sets many expectations in the listeners.

Structuring a P3O

A P3O must offer support to the project organisation. It will need a structure that matches the organisation and its needs. Earlier in the book, the P3M model was introduced as an interface between the differing world views of corporate strategy and project implementation. A P3O structure needs to mirror this. It needs to have an interface which works with and supports the Portfolios, interfacing with strategy. It also needs to have an interface which supports the Projects. Typically Programmes will link most strongly with the Project interface. Finally, it needs a strong "backbone" of skills and expertise to promote good practice and to draw upon in the supporting functions.

The "interfaces" generate outputs which the organisation needs. Typically, the P3O is involved where it is more efficient to generate material once and reuse it across the organisation. This could include templates to represent good practice or compliance. This might perhaps cover documents, standardised reports or training. For example by agreeing and centralising project reports, there will be a reduction in cost of development, a better ability to communicate, and an opportunity for sharing reports which could lead to identifying new good practice.

To be effective the P3O must deliver value, not just volume. This means the P3O must interface effectively with the organisation to identify what is really valued. The interfaces must be effective in supporting both standards and variations, giving value without being constraining. The PMO must also be built around a strong "Centre of Excellence" backbone with the skills and knowledge to identify good practice both within and outside the organisation.

Strategy   Implementation

Figure 31 – Components of a P3O

> *One challenge is the balance of standards and variations. Standardising an approach across groups will generally lead to some efficiency gains. There can be sharing in documentation, tools and training costs. It may also lead to some increase in quality as good practices are shared. But this can only go so far. Different groups will have different needs. Standardisation can over-constrain, limiting a group's effectiveness. You need a mechanism to support the independence of each group in creating variations on the basic theme. This can be a hard balance to get right.*
>
> *The balance can be hard to assess at the start. Typically each group has their own practices. They will often have locally optimised them, so their own approach is polished as well as it can be. There may be gains to be made by adopting a different approach but the migration will have a cost. It may result in a worse situation for some period. Local optimisation is one of the biggest barriers to adopting standardisation, even when the long term benefits are visible.*

The three year rule

Is just creating a P3O going to solve all your problems? Sadly, as you will have suspected, it's not that easy. A mechanism for delivery of successful project approaches is necessary, but having one does not guarantee successful approaches or their delivery. Many studies have shown that organisations create P3Os/PMOs and then find they add little value.

The PMI's "Pulse of the Profession" report 2015 suggested 76% of high performing organisations had a project management office. Sounds good – maybe the PMO is an asset... But these were also present in 64% of low performing organisations. There's not much difference between those two figures. Creating a P3O/PMO does not seem to be a differentiator which will itself ensure a measure of success.

The lifespan of PMOs is frequently quite short. Many organisations experiment with such a structure, find it achieves little and disband it. The literature frequently refers to a three or four year cycle of formation and disbanding. Indeed the idea of this short cycle has become quite established wisdom among PMOs.

> *the research indicated that over 75% of organizations that set up a PMO shut it down within 3 years because it didn't demonstrate any added value.*
>
> **M. Stanleigh - From Crisis to Control (2006)**

Mere creation of a structure doesn't seem to be enough. There's a piece of the puzzle still missing. If building an organisational structure that is capable of delivering isn't the whole answer, what else do we need?

Continuous improvement

There is no perfect project solution. Managing projects is not something which your organisation will "solve" and then move on. It will never be possible to create an approach for running projects, apply that approach and find that it works perfectly, now and always. Hopefully that is not too disappointing a message. There are many project methodologies which give this comforting illusion. Companies may feel that if they just buy into a specific methodology (generally one with an adequately thick book or highly paid consultants) this will solve all of their problems for ever.

The truth is rather more complex. As we have seen, organisations evolve. Today's project solution may not be correct for tomorrow when the organisation is larger and more complex. Investing huge effort in a project approach for today may or may not succeed but it will certainly not guarantee that you can still deliver projects effectively next year.

A new project approach also cannot simply be implemented as a whole. The organisation cannot typically accommodate so high a level of change, especially while also delivering the existing projects. It is necessary to build up capability over a period of time, familiarizing people with each change.

Adopting a specific, documented methodology may make adoption easier. This can help with clarity of the end goal and the required component parts. But the most critical process for successfully adopting a project approach is what is known as "Continuous Improvement". However good the initial implementation, the ability to improve the implementation is vital to success.

Continuous Improvement always reminds me of Aesop's story of the tortoise and the hare. However good an initial change you put in place, this will always eventually be overtaken by incremental improvement over a period of time.

The challenge is to keep people focussed. The initial improvement is a very visible step. Change is attractive and it's easy to think the problem is then "solved". On-going continuous improvement by contrast may just seem like hard work.

Culture is a critical area here as in so much of your project approach. Continuous Improvement isn't a natural way of working and needs support and nurturing. It is much easier for people to keep working the way they always have done. If the organisation wishes to improve it needs to be actively promoting improvement. This means moving away from a crisis-driven viewpoint. Although there will be times the organisation must address crises, improvement may be less urgent but no less important.

Hero culture tends to be in direct opposition to a continuous improvement approach. Heroes seek out large dramatic events and major changes as a backdrop for their success. Improvement is about the incremental effect of small change over a large timeframe. Hero culture also emphasizes the role of key individuals while improvement is inclusive and pulls in knowledge from all. The problem is that hero culture is attractive and builds good stories, which are communicated around the organisation. To promote improvement, you must find a similar way of selling the successes of an incremental approach.

I have found constant communication is key to keeping improvement in people's minds. Whenever new ideas come out of teams, you need to make sure these are visible. Often the team themselves don't even realise what they have found is new. Coach the teams so that they learn that they are innovating and show them how what they have is what others need.

Teams can present their ideas or can be encouraged to use social media. There are many opportunities such as blogging about their ideas. Management presentations and blogs should give visibility to changes and improvements as well as to direct revenue. The overall goal is to promote the belief that teams are empowered to create change, that change is valued and that it is normal for teams to generate improvements themselves not to wait for others to institute "change programmes".

Learning

For continuous improvement to work well, you first need ideas. Many (perhaps most) of the good improvement ideas come not from managers or consultants but from the people who are actually working on projects. So you need a pathway for change which listens to the individuals and captures their ideas. Several names are used for the forum for capturing project learnings. They are sometimes called "Postmortems" from the concept of analysis of a project after closure (perhaps a too negative name). Or they can be "Lessons Learned" (although strictly they aren't learned at this point, just identified). I like the Agile term "Retrospective" which to me captures the idea that this is looking back at what *has* happened as a balance to planning which looks forward at what *will* happen.

So capturing ideas and learning from what you have done is a starting point. You need to learn from what went well and especially from what went less well. And here another cultural issue comes into play. If something goes badly on a project there are three responses which may occur. And how the organisation responds tells you a significant amount about the organisation's maturity.

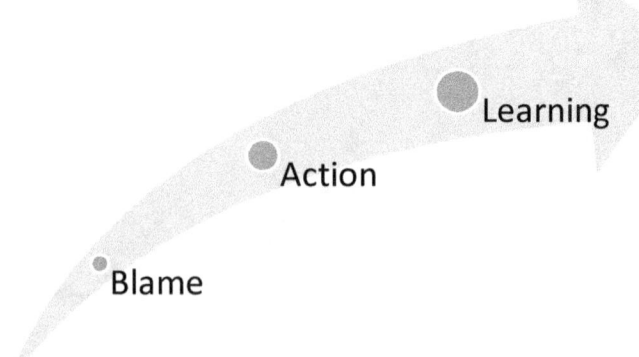

Figure 32 – Response to set-backs

Blame.

In a fear-based culture, the response to a project failure is to blame others. Since safety is paramount, the team will seek to find explanations which remove their own accountability for failure. If the focus is to find specific explanations rather than to understand the truth it is unlikely that there will be much learning involved. Worse still, since the team are looking for an explanation in which they are not accountable, they will not feel that they should make changes for the future. A blame culture pushes teams to believe that any solution is outside their control because that means the problem is outside their accountability.

Action

In the action response, the team rallies around fixing the immediate issue. Everyone works long hours, the crisis is solved and then the team gets back to normal working. This is far preferable to just finding someone to blame. But there is little thought given to how to prevent the recurrence of the crisis. The lack of learning is because of a belief that crises are inevitable. The focus here is on *corrective* action which addresses today's problem, not *preventative* measures to ensure that the problem does not recur.

Learning

In a learning response, although the immediate problem is still fixed, the team continues to consider how to avoid a recurrence. The first step here is to consider *why* something went wrong. The team need some deep analysis to get beyond the symptoms to the underlying cause. By abstracting the issue to the "lesson" behind it, the team can see how it could be prevented next time. This isn't easy. The analysis can need some skill and facilitation. And it can be painful for a team to admit that errors have been made as they explore how to prevent them in the future.

These three attitudes can be very deeply ingrained. And changing or evolving the culture between these is a challenge that may take many years. I would say that most of the teams with which I have worked have been "action oriented". This can be a very attractive environment. There is a lot of excitement around handling immediate issues and many people enjoy working this way. Further, the organisation can feel too stretched to invest in a learning approach. It can even seem rather dull and perhaps inefficient. Focussing more on action seems to mean more outputs, more successes and so a growing company. But past a certain point this ceases to scale. The endless crises impact quality and customer satisfaction. Eventually even the most enthusiastic team members get tired of the repeated errors, or burn out from the overwork.

Which response do you tend to see in your organisation? Blame, Action or Learning? Of course there will be some of each but often one is culturally very strong. Are you comfortable with the response and do you find it effective?

Learning case Study – Model 299

In the 1930s Boeing bid for a contract to build a long-range bombers for the US Army Air Corps. Their design, the Model 299, looked like a great success. It could fly further and faster than previous bombers, and carry far more bombs than had been originally specified.

The final test flight was held on October 30th 1935. It was little more than a formality before the contract was confirmed. In the test, the aircraft made a normal takeoff but then stalled and fell, bursting into flames upon impact.

What happened?

The investigation found "pilot error" as the cause of the crash. The pilot had neglected to release the elevator lock prior to take off. This had caused a stall which resulted in the crash.

Boeing lost the contract, which went to Douglas. The newspapers summed up the Model 299 as:

too much airplane for one man to fly

Why did this happen?

The test pilot had been the U.S. Army Air Corps' Chief of Flight Testing. He certainly didn't lack experience. But the aircraft was complex. Relying on memory to complete all of the tasks was not enough to prevent error. Boeing considered different approaches for dealing with this problem. Training didn't seem to be the answer, and neither was technical change to the aircraft. It far outperformed its competitors in technical capability.

The solution which they adopted was a pilot's checklist. Four checklists were eventually developed - takeoff, flight, before landing, and after landing. Rather than rely on the pilots remembering the key activities, they used a reference checklist to ensure that everything was done correctly in the right sequence.

Boeing developed 12 prototype 'B-17' planes. With the checklists and rigorous training, the 12 aircraft managed to fly 1.8 million miles without a serious accident. The U.S. Army eventually ordered over 12 thousand of the aircraft which became one of the key bombers of the Second World War.

Checklists are now standard across aviation.

What can we learn?

How often have you been distracted and missed something? Maybe something so obvious that you couldn't believe you had missed it. Whenever you focus intently on a task, it's easy to make mistakes, often "trivial" in nature but sometimes with a major impact. And this extends to projects. When a project team is focused on the complex tasks involved in making the project outputs, they can easily make relatively basic errors.

A key part of the continuous improvement process is to build the knowledge base of avoidable errors. This is where checklists can play a role, in the same way as for aviation. A checklist will not increase a team member's skill and allow him or her to create higher performing outputs. The B-17 checklist didn't make the plane fly further or faster. A checklist will not manage teams, communicate with stakeholders or make decisions. These are all critical project areas that individuals must perform. However what it will do is ensure that while the team perform these critical functions they do not make errors which could have been predicted and avoided.

To make checklists effective they need to integrate into the improvement culture. Whenever an error occurs, or a potential error is avoided, the team need a mechanism to capture the learning and ensure that future errors are avoided. The checklist mechanism is effective here, if three basic principles are ensured:

- Time is spent to identify the underlying root cause of each problem
- A means of preventing the cause is logged in the checklist system
- The updated checklist is used by future projects to ensure the risk has been addressed

Longer term there is also a fourth principle which is very important and frequently challenging to implement.

- The checklist environment is managed so that old checks are removed when no longer relevant.

I have seen checklists work very effectively as an integrated part of ensuring the quality of project outcomes. However, there was a lot of "behind the scenes" work to make it successful. A key part of this is in ensuring that teams look beyond fixing an issue and think about how it might be prevented. And then there is compliance work to ensure that the checklists are being used effectively on all projects.

Perhaps the biggest challenge proved to be keeping the checklists relevant. Experience showed that too many questions, or questions which did not apply to a specific project, caused problems. A short and relevant checklist would focus a team on assessing risk. But beyond a certain size, the checklist rapidly became seen as an administrative overhead. The quality of responses and level of consideration fell off rapidly. We found this occurred at about 15 questions, or if more than about 10-20% of questions did not directly apply to the project.

As a consequence, significant overhead was needed to "prune" and refresh checklists. This needs to be seen as part of the continual improvement process, which is not about adding process, but about ensuring the process is always relevant.

Finding time for improvement

There is never a "right time" to make changes. Project teams will not suddenly find the time to improve. Continuous improvement must be planned, as the name suggests, to be continuous. If changes are incremental and driven from project learning, time must be set aside to learn. And this time is needed both to find the learnings and to apply them as improvements. This will never be easy. As we saw when discussing roadmaps in Chapter 6, people will tend to focus on the urgent rather than the important. By its nature, improvement activity is rarely the most urgent problem. And it can often find that it is deferred. Often indefinitely.

There will be crises in the organisation. And so there will be times when non-critical activities need to be deprioritized. At these times, resource will be taken off improvements in order to manage the business. But the converse of this is that when the immediate crises have reduced, the work on improvement must resume. As a master in the field puts this:

> *The most important thing about doing kaizen (continuous improvement) is to do kaizen when times are good, the economy is strong, and the company is profitable*
>
> *Taiichi Ohno*

This is paradoxical. When all is going smoothly an organisation can easily become less focused on improvement. Why spend effort on improvement when you are already doing well? Surely you improve when you see problems and failures. But when you see the urgent need, you are focused on managing the problem and may lack the resources to progress improvement. Building in incremental improvement, especially in the good times, is critical to having an effective project approach.

How do you make this happen? There are a myriad of distractions and improvement is rarely the most urgent function (as we discussed under "Portfolios", urgency is different from importance). So how do you raise its profile? Firstly you can increase the visibility of active improvement activities. Do you know how much time is spent on these? Or who is working on them? If you want to ensure that this work happens you will have to measure and prioritise.

Measuring time

The first key is to understand how much effort is being spent on improvement. Intent is not enough and you will need to know how the intent is translating into reality. Is the improvement work always pushed off the list by crises? You need to decide how much you want to spend and ensure that you are tracking the real effort against the intent. You may well find initially that your good intentions are resulting in surprisingly little actual time spent. But the first step is to discover where you are.

Top down support

Improvement activities need top down support. For any change programme this legitimizes the work and makes budget and effort available. Visible support for improvement from the organisational leaders is important in ensuring that teams feel valued and supported in investing time in the work. However, top-down support is not typically sufficient to make improvement activity successful. Trying to enforce improvement simply by measuring time spent and punishing failure to improve will not be a successful approach.

Viral adoption

Top-down support gives empowerment. But it is horizontal (or "grassroots") support which drives adoption. Successful improvements come from the practitioners. They succeed because they are relevant. Improvement needs to engage the teams involved. Often this is more of a challenge than top-down support. Management may agree a change will lead to benefits, but engaging the practitioners means persuading the people who have to change.

This is where P3Os can often fail. They have to interface well with the organisation and use the "Center of Excellence" skills to understand what brings value to the projects. A P3O should produce outputs not because it can but because the project teams want to use them. Otherwise you risk a "Crisis of Red Tape" situation where the P3O justifies its existence by volume of output alone.

Viral adoption needs the practitioners to become the evangelists for the change. For this to happen they must see the benefits, and they must also be given a platform or a voice to sell the benefits to others. Rather than a change being imposed you want teams to be *asking* to adopt the change.

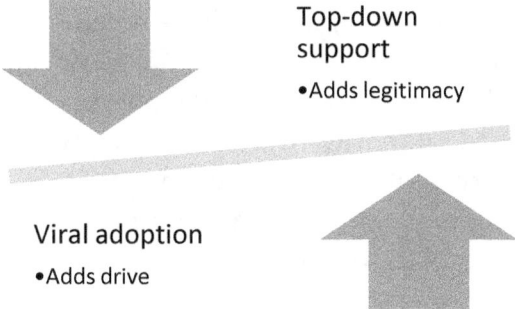

Figure 33 – Combining top down and bottom up change

Chapter 10

Keeping projects on track

For projects to work well, you need an effective governance structure. Governance is needed for the strategic/portfolio level to be able to ensure that the projects are being effective at delivering value. For example the portfolio needs to know that projects are well-run, will be able to deliver within the assigned resources, and will deliver the expected benefits, to the expected quality, at the expected time.

Governance is also important for the projects themselves. The benefits of governance to the project team are often forgotten. For a project to be empowered, it must have an effective governance system. This may sound contradictory, for a governance system may seem to take power away from the project. But for a project team to exercise authority it must know what authority it possesses. Otherwise it will either be too timid to make decisions, constantly trying to pass them to an external authority, or it will clash with the rest of the organisation.

I have often seen project managers say "I can't make that decision as I don't have the authority". But the same project managers may not be able to ensure the decision is made elsewhere. If the governance structure is defined, it is then clear where the authority does reside. It can be a damaging situation if managers are both unwilling to decide themselves and are also unsure where the authority to make that decision resides. The worst situation is they may have the accountability for the decision but not empowerment to take the decision.

What do we mean by governance? A dictionary definition would be as below.

> *Governance: The action or manner of governing a state, organization*
>
> **Oxford English Dictionary**

Clearly this is a fairly general definition which doesn't align with business usage. Governing a state is not a usual situation in an organisational context. What we mean here is more specific to an organisation. The definition below is clearer.

> *Governance is the control framework through which programmes deliver their ... objectives and remain within corporate visibility and control*
>
> ***Managing Successful Programmes - Axelos***

Governing Board

Governance is the set of controls which run through the layers. This joins the organisational strategic layer to the implementation project layer. Governance then is what ensures that the layered model works in implementing the organisational needs.

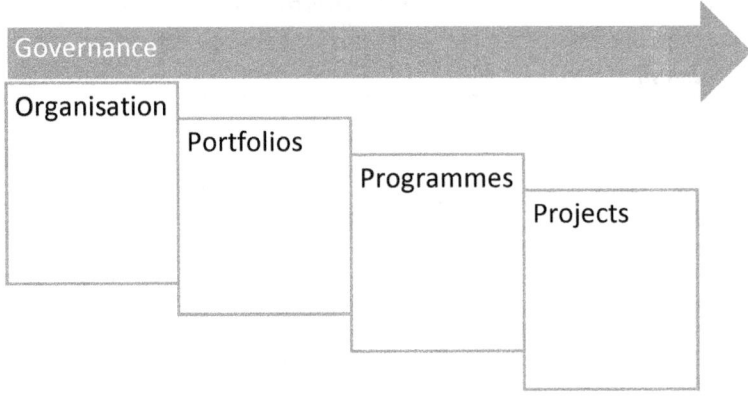

Figure 34 – P3M model and governance

The layered model of P3M is ideal for a governance structure. Each level creates the level below and then forms a guiding "board" to keep them aligned. For example, projects are created by a programme to achieve specific goals. The programme doesn't then ignore the projects, and it's important that this is recognised. Instead the programme becomes a "Project Board" to guide the projects.

It is dangerously easy to bypass this model. Even if on paper the project is owned by a programme, it is easy to have effective control elsewhere. This could be functional owners, who typically manage the resources on the project. Or it might be technology specialists who architect the solutions. Or the project could be heavily influenced by reactive marketing requests for new features.

The role of the project board is to:

Define and delegate authority

Authority is delegated to the project team to ensure that the project team have the authority and control of budget and resourcing necessary to proceed on a day-to-day basis. But authority remains with the board for certain key agreed gates and decisions.

Resolve strategic issues

Where questions lie outside the understanding of the project team, because they lie in the area of expertise or authority of the programme, the project board can be used by the project team to resolve issues.

Assure the integrity of value and the business plan

The project board create and own the business plan for the project. This ensures that if the project delivers what has been requested, the organisation will gain the desired value. This is important to allow the project team to concentrate on delivering as requested.

Form an escalation path

As the key linkage upwards from the project towards the organisation leadership, the project board allows the project team to escalate any issues which lie outside their delegated authority.

How does project governance work in your organisation? Is the project board clearly defined for each project? And how does it tie in with the other levels of the model? Is there a clear flow where business strategy integrates with the board controlling each individual project? And how well do you feel this works "on the ground"?

Lifecycles

Project gating is a key part of effective governance. The project board delegates budget and authority for a stage of the project with a requirement to deliver explicit value from the stage. The project team then reports back on completion of the stage. This allows review of status and progress and ensures that project, programme and portfolio layers remain aligned. It also allows a degree of tailoring. Since the project board represent the business case, they have an opportunity for flexibility which is lacking at the project level. Should the outputs from a project stage not be achieving the expected value for the organisation, the programme or portfolio layers can intervene, changing the project parameters as appropriate.

Projects generally implement a lifecycle. In some organisations the stages will be clearly defined. This is especially true of highly regulated industries where the state of the project will have significant, probably legally-enforced, implications. For example, the diagram below is a simple model for a medical device lifecycle.

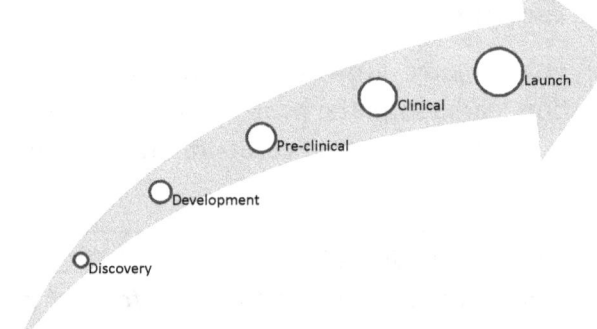

Figure 35 – Hypothetical medical device lifecycle

In general most projects will run through a simple and generic lifecycle. The project lifecycle can be made into a general model fairly easily. Projects typically to run through five separate stages with extensions or subdivisions according to the technology used.

When designing a project approach, keep this structure in mind. You want to ensure that these stages are represented in some form. The actual names, of course, are not important as long as everyone understands what happens in each stage.

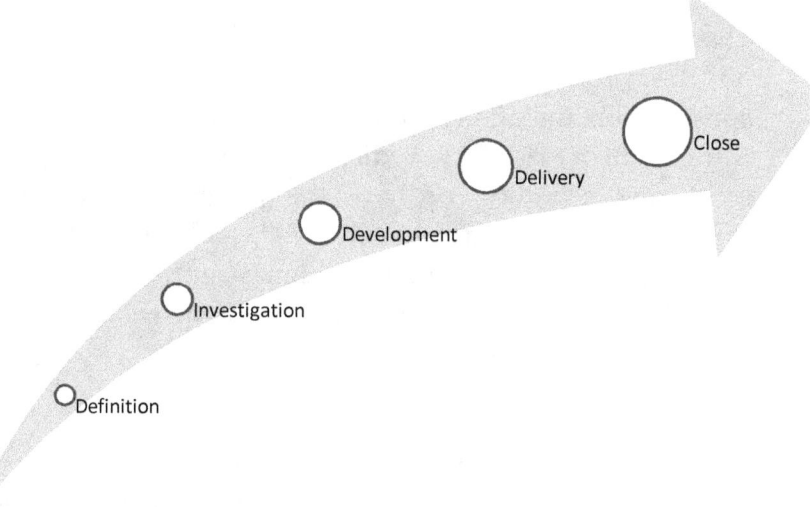

Figure 36 – Simple project lifecycle

What project lifecycle are you using? Most importantly does it work for the teams? Does everyone understand each stage, what it is for and how it is used? If you started again from a blank sheet would you create the same lifecycle?

Definition stage

This is focussed on ensuring that the objectives of the project are understood. In particular the definition stage is the handover from the higher levels of the P3M model. The project needs to be on a firm foundation with everyone involved agreed what constitutes "success". This requires a clear definition of business case and governance. Projects are far more likely to succeed without the conflict inherent from different stakeholders having different ideas of what the desired outcome may be.

Investigation stage

This stage looks at how the objectives will be achieved. Depending on the project this may mean the creation of a detailed specification, the signing of contractual supplier agreements or the completion of feasibility studies. At the end of this stage there is a solid understanding of how the project will be addressed, including people and roles involved, and the approaches to be used. Completing the investigation stage means that the team have demonstrated that they can achieve the value to the business specified in the business case.

Development stage

In this stage the project outputs are produced. This could vary from physical objects to a new tool or a change process being implemented through the project. "Project outputs" refers to any items which are created as a mechanism to deliver the value from the project. At the end of the stage the work has been done and the output complete. However at this point the outputs are available but have not been used.

Delivery stage

Once developed, the project output must be delivered or used. This could be a near-trivial upload of software to a server. Or it could be a complex interaction with an extensive user base over a long time period. For a change project this is the conversion of a capability into an outcome, moving from the potential for change to a valuable result.

Close stage

Finally the project should close. Projects are bounded and will end with an assessment of the delivered outputs, both in terms of completeness against the specification and in terms of value delivered. Was the project a success against the initial criteria and what can be learned from the project? Issues should be subjected to root cause analysis to understand what truly occurred. Lessons from this project should be made available to be fed forwards to future projects. This is a key point for organisational learning.

Gates

How do you transition from one stage to the next? Each transition is not in the control of the project team and is a point where they need to seek external authorisation. Any time when authority to proceed is outside the project team, we refer to this as a "gate". Gates are the control points in the project where it is agreed in advance that the project will not proceed without approval. This is a powerful control mechanism. Gating allows the project team to run relatively independently between gates with the knowledge that there will be an in-depth assessment of project status at the gating points.

Figure 37 – Gated lifecycle

Gates are controlled by the project board. The board represents the programme authority which owns the business case for the project. The board is therefore best placed to assess the progress of the project and necessary interventions. The involvement of the project board in gates is important to ensure that the assessment is not only on project progress against planned outputs but against outcomes and value for the organisation. There may be shifts in the external environment which impact the business case and the awareness of these can most effectively be brought to the gating by the board, representing the programme layer.

Plans

"Where is the plan?" seems a simple question. But it can sum up the tension between the different levels of the P3M model. In many organisations planning is an area of conflict. Let's consider why planning is such a problem area. As with many problems this is often a communication issue and is grounded in the lack of consistent project language across the organisation. As we have seen, "portfolio/strategy" language and concepts are often different from "project" language. This can lead to a conversation which goes as follows:

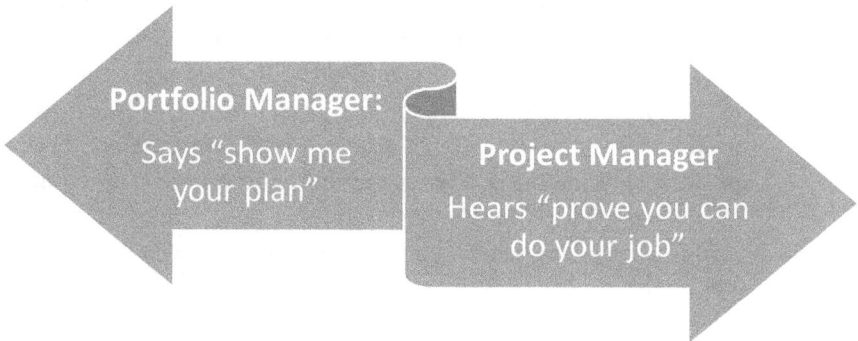

Figure 38 – Language and plans

The project team may feel challenged or threatened. They often respond by generating increasing volumes of reports, metrics and (all too often) Gantt charts. If these have value, that's good. But all too often neither the project team nor the strategist needs these. The project team generates these artefacts because they are accepted "currency" to prove that they are in control. But they don't actually use them to control the project. And they don't necessarily give the roadmap owner the information that he or she needs. So they become at best pointless and at worst a large administrative drain on the team.

I worked with a small software team who had recently been added to a larger group. They were a highly customer-focussed responsive team that used an agile sprint-based approach to manage their projects. And they were successful – they made good revenue and their customers respected them.

I found that every week someone manually copied their current status from their Agile tool into a scheduling tool and made a Gantt chart of the schedule. This and the forward planning was manually documented in a presentation tool. And of course, next iteration there was enough change this all had to be manually regenerated from scratch.

I asked them why they did this. Was this some legacy from their past? The answer was that the group they now belonged to kept asking for "plans". And the only thing that seemed to satisfy the new group was Gantt charts and presentations. These weren't used by the team, and didn't give any real information about the project. When I asked the group management why they needed this data, the response was that this was what all the other projects generated and they "needed to be confident".

Gate review culture

If you as a leader ask for a plan, what is your intent and what do you expect to see? At a strategic or Portfolio management level, you are developing a roadmap which is delivered by others. The roadmap is your plan, and your accountability, and you want to be confident that it will be delivered successfully. When you are involved in a gate review, you want to understand status and planning. So when you ask for a plan, what does this really mean?

> "Show me the plan" = "How confident does the planning make us in the delivery of the roadmap?"

I use "planning" not "plan". You are reviewing the planning more than the look and feel of a specific artefact. The outputs help you understand the plan, the planning approach and how the objectives will be achieved. But an offline review of a project schedule file is rarely a substitute for an open discussion of what the project challenges are and how these are being addressed.

It is important to make sure that nothing has been missed. You will need to step through the planning in quite a staged way, looking at the requirements and how these are addressed in the planning. It's easy to miss something basic when planning. A fresh pair of eyes from a reviewer can be a real asset.

Remember to check that the plan covers the full scope of the project. Sometimes when reviewing projects whole deliverables have been missing because the team aren't aware of them or don't feel responsible for them. I recall one plan which had no mention of customer-facing documentation or any delivery of the product, the team saying they had made a "software development" plan. Sometimes as in this case, discussing the plan can tell you a lot about the team and how they see the project.

Review culture

A plan review assesses whether enough planning has been done to have a low level of risk. Everyone involved has a different focus and knowledge base and each reviewer may notice something different which is missing from a plan. This could be a requirement that had been missed, an output which is omitted, an assumption made or an issue to be resolved.

Reviews must be collaborative not competitive. The project team must feel that the review helps them by noticing things that they have missed and that this will increase their chance of success. This then encourages them to be open in presenting the plan.

Good plan review builds over time. For me, plan review has always been part of an ongoing coaching relationship. With an inexperienced planner on a simpler project, you may just go through the basics. But as coaching relationships develop, you can explore the approach and mindset in more detail. The starting point becomes "what is different about this project and how are you addressing it?" Some of my most enjoyable times at ChipCo were reviewing plans, looking at the likely failure points, discussing how these were being addressed

Too often reviewers at gating points look to "trim" the project. The plan may be more expensive or longer than desired and there is a huge temptation to "review" the plan to make it more attractive, not more realistic. With this attitude the review becomes a confrontation. The team is encouraged to exaggerate or to conceal while the reviewer is encouraged to trivialise or intimidate.

This is especially true if the reviewer is also the resource manager. In my experience this combination of roles risks a significant conflict of interest. A resource manager will have a pool of resources to cover multiple projects. They are typically incentivised to resource successfully as many projects as possible. But they are often not rewarded for project success. Faced with a large project estimate which risks exceeding his or her capacity to supply resource, they will often "push back" on estimates to get projects to fit a pre-determined envelope of available resource. If they have no "stake" in the viability of the project this can leave the project in a critically under-resourced state at the gate. Rather than the review helping the business, it can ensure that projects are doomed from the start.

 Think about when you are involved in plan reviews. How often do you start with a willingness to accept the team's outcome? Or how often do you already have an idea of the "right" answer and a desire to shape the plan to fit what you want?

The primary purpose of a review is to identify items missed by the planner which could increase project risk. As such a successful plan review would be expected to increase, not decrease, cost and schedule.

Planning Horizon

One way to assess the planning uncertainty is to look at the level to which the work are broken down. It is a well understood planning concept that a single long task has much higher uncertainty than the same activity broken into several short tasks. This is primarily because of the complexity which is removed in the breakdown as smaller tasks are more clearly defined and less uncertain. By breaking an 8 week task into eight 1 week tasks we have added some information about how the task will be approached and so reduced the overall uncertainty.

It is a fallacy that any project will have a detailed breakdown of every activity at the start. Even the most sequential project will need to learn as it progresses. You want the plan to be complete, so you want to include, not ignore, items that may not be well understood.

An understanding of the planning could be seen from the distribution of task sizes. What would you expect to see? Well, that needs to match the project is run. For an iterative project you might see that all of the activities to be worked on in the next iteration were well broken down into a manageable level of detail. The next stage of activities are thought about at a higher level. For a more sequentially planned project you are likely to see most tasks quite well broken down with some of the further forward tasks still large and requiring investigation before they can be decomposed.

This chart comes from a project that I was reviewing as part of a coaching discussion around planning. The team were finding it difficult to communicate their plan and as a result faced the assumption that they had no plan. There was some discussion within the team about the quality of planning. They had spent some time working on identifying and breaking down tasks and felt that this had been worthwhile. But they were failing to communicate this level of work. So we decided to show the distribution of tasks in the project in graphical form. But what did that mean? Did it suggest a "good" level of planning or not?

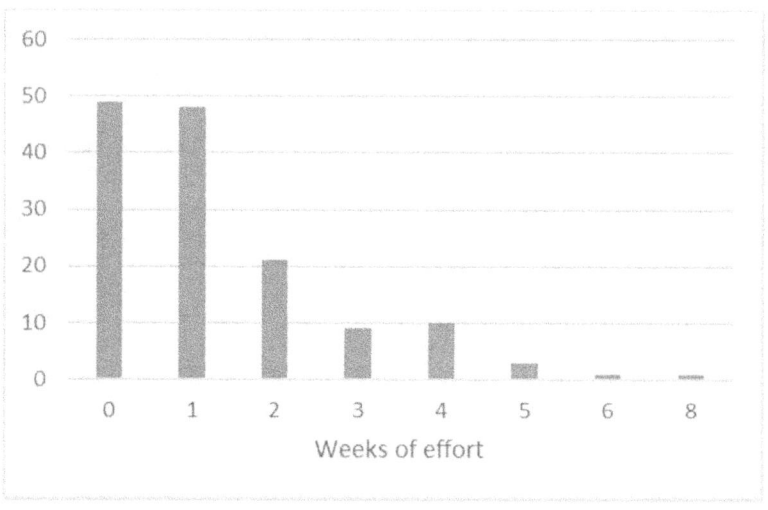

Figure 39 – Task distribution histogram

As a reviewer, you need to assess whether this breakdown of tasks is adequate to understand and manage the project. The larger tasks are less well understood and so represent a level of risk to the project. Perhaps ideally the whole project would have been broken down into small tasks. But this might suggest a level of initial investigation which could be prohibitively time-consuming.

Inevitably there will be a mix of more and less well estimated activities. Typically the closer activities will be more broken down and some of the further-forward activities will still lack definition. For a rolling replanning approach (rather than formal iteration) the task distribution could be expected to be exponential in shape, with a fall-off in number as you move to the larger, less well defined tasks. Iterative projects might be expected to have a clear separation between "planned" and "backlog" work.

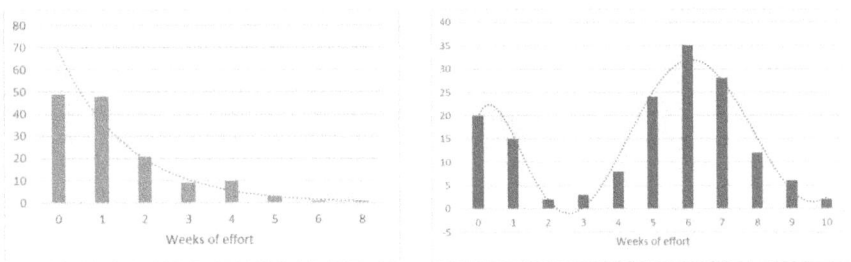

Figure 40 – Task distribution exponential or bimodal

Managing a gate assessment

A gate assessment is not just a tick against plan completion. At first glance it might appear that a simple check is sufficient. After all, the project created a plan of what it intended to complete by this point. It would seem adequate simply to check that the expected plan is complete and then to sign off the stage. However, this devalues the assessment process. A gate is not just a reporting measure that states that the project has reached a certain point. Any gate satisfies a range of purposes as shown in the diagram below. And as shown in this diagram, the different purposes indicate a level of maturity in the gating process.

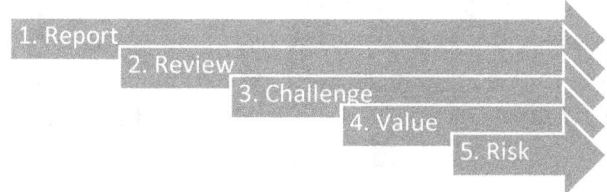

Figure 41 – Gating maturity levels

Reporting

Any gate must satisfy a reporting requirement. This is the lowest level of value from a gate. The defined point in the project flow is a good occasion to ensure that the project status is well understood and communicated to all stakeholders. This may involve a distributed report, but ideally involves a meeting and a presentation. It is a chance for the project team to explain their view of where the project truly is at this point. Gates should be respected and the key stakeholders should attend and listen to the project team's status update. The key outcome should be that at the end of the gate everyone has a common, accurate understanding of the status of the project.

Don't underestimate the value of a simple gate report. Especially when this is presented at a meeting, not just a circulated report. I have been at gate reviews where it is clear that those present have radically different interpretations of what the project is producing and when. You should never get to that point, but the gate meeting does reset and align expectations which may have drifted substantially.

Review

Each gate is intended as a review point. Simply reporting is not sufficient for a high quality gate. It should be planned to review the project status against the expected status. To be effective this means that the gate should be scheduled to occur at a clearly defined point in the project. You should be clear what is expected at this point, and this should be measurable. Gates therefore should be part of the planning – what outputs are expected, what quality they have achieved, what measurements will be used to assess that quality and what results are expected from the measurements. The team should be presenting the facts and the variances from the plan.

Project review at gates is powerful if the company culture supports it. But it's also too easy for a defensive team to cover their tracks and only present positive data. This helps no-one, neither the business which needs to understand the real status of the project, nor the team who will eventually be caught out by the facts. Mostly I have been fortunate to work in low blame cultures where teams are able to present the true project status without fear of consequences.

Some teams have been rather optimistic about status. This has often been through lack of experience rather than dishonesty. Other teams have been defensive and sometimes even omitted key data to attempt to look good. When building a gating structure into an organisation, it is important to emphasise that the first of these, optimism, is a sign of inexperience, but the second must be clearly unacceptable. The gating process should be about a shared understanding, not a reward or a transfer of blame.

On one occasion we had a project team which had come to a gate apparently having completed everything expected. Their local management supported them that the project was on track and running to schedule. Investigation at the gate approval discovered a less rosy picture. Although the team had completed all of the testing and quality checks, these had raised a large number of areas of necessary rework. In order to appear on track, the team had marked all of the testing and reviewing as done and kept the failures and resulting rework "off plan" on a separate action list. This had grown to a huge backlog and the project turned out to be three months behind where it claimed to be. A project in this state was always going to fail at some point. By catching this at the gate it was recoverable (if painful). The team's failure was not in falling behind or in introducing too many defects – they were quite a junior team and were struggling with the design. The real failure was in the team (and especially their management) attempting to hide the true situation.

Challenge

A gate is not just a presentation from the team. To be effective, gates must represent a level of challenge to the team's thinking. It is very easy for a team to have the mind-set that a particular approach will be effective, or that an issue can be ignored. Gates rely on the attendees bringing their own viewpoint and contributing this.   Many studies have shown the risks of Groupthink – the tendency of teams to adopt a common viewpoint and to be reluctant to challenge this.

Groupthink can make quite unrealistic views go unchallenged within the group. A gate is an opportunity for those from outside the team to question assumptions and ideas which may be fundamental to the team's way of working. The stakeholders should leave the gate meeting feeling not only that they understand the status of the project but also that the true status has been evaluated.

Bringing in genuine challenge at gates can be difficult. When I was attending gating assessments, I used to muse about how this could possibly work. The project team have checked everything carefully. They have prepared all the reports which they are presenting. And they are familiar with all the detail of the project. How can an "outsider" ask questions that really challenge this? And yet over and over we saw the value of external assessment.

One example was a pre-release gate. The team were ready to deliver in a few days. They put up a list of the release activities which they had to complete. And one of them was to finish writing a set of tests. The assessors asked why the project was ready for release if the testing wasn't complete. The answer was that the tests could be completed and run the night before release. The tests "were sure to pass", and were seen as part of releasing, not as part of testing the product.

By having external assessors we could challenge what was clearly a case of groupthink by the team. The project wasn't quite where the team imagined, because of the likelihood that the unfinished tests would raise issues which would require rework and a repeat of the release process. We could reset expectations for the availability of the product.

The tests did indeed flag up issues and the release was indeed delayed. The external challenge in the gate had anticipated this issue and ensured that action was taken to plan for the delay.

Value

The stakeholders should ensure that the project is doing the right thing for the organisation. This is a level beyond just challenging whether the project is on track to deliver what was originally intended. By having the project board involved in the gate, the focus can go beyond the original planned outputs of the project. The gate can also consider whether the project remains on track to deliver the intended value to the business. The mapping between project outputs and organisational value may change over time. It may become clear that further outputs are needed, or that changes in specification are required. The return on some outputs may have diminished, while others may have increased to the extent that further project funding would be advisable. The gate gives an opportunity to bring together the project team, with their intimate knowledge of the status and plans, with the stakeholders, with their awareness of the business case, the organisational value and any shifts in the environment.

Risk

At the highest level of maturity a gate becomes a risk assessment. It is easy to see a gate as a pass or fail check on the project. Gates are often managed as though what is needed is a "tick" from more senior members of the organisation. The gate is then passed and forgotten about. A far more valuable way of looking at a gate is as an assessment of risk. There will be variance between the plan and the real status, there will be changes in external factors and there will be issues exposed by the challenge from the stakeholders. Rather than these preventing the gate from being "passed", they can be seen in the context of risk level on the project. Few projects will have exactly kept to the plan. What is important is how the project team will be ensuring the plan continues to be successful.

Risk-based assessment was the hardest part of gating to ensure. Managers are often more comfortable with "black and white" decisions. When a project comes to a gate with nearly everything complete, the easy solution is to ask them to come back when everything is complete. We saw many cases of project boards refusing to sign off a gate because of minor areas where the planned work wasn't quite completed.

The problem was that there were only one or two items at fault. No-one was willing to agree that the gate could be passed, but also no-one was willing to delay the next stage. The result was an impasse meaning that in those teams the gate lost much relevance. Projects would proceed as though the gate was passed, but without an agreed sign off. Gates often wouldn't be approved until the next gate was reached.

The teams who understood risk-based assessment tended to have very well prepared presentations. They would say what the variance from the plan was, when the outstanding items could be completed, what the action plan was and what the level of risk was. When approving a gate, you knew exactly what decision you were making.

Chapter 11

Conclusion

It is not impossible to build a successful project organisation. It will seem challenging, even daunting, at this stage. But many organisations have successfully built effective project approaches.

However, the statistics on failing projects show that it isn't easy and that many organisations struggle. There will be challenges along the way. We have seen some of the problems in this book along with some suggestions about how you might address them.

At a top level the formula for success is clear. The message is well described in the quote below:

> *"It's quite simple" I said.*
> *"We focused relentlessly on delivering for customers.*
>
> *We set ourselves some simple aims,*
> *and some basic values to live by.*
>
> *And we then created a process to achieve them,*
> *making sure everyone knew what they were responsible for".*
>
> **Terry Leahy, "Management in 10 words"**

To build a project organisation you need to focus relentlessly on the basics. I could break this down into key steps.

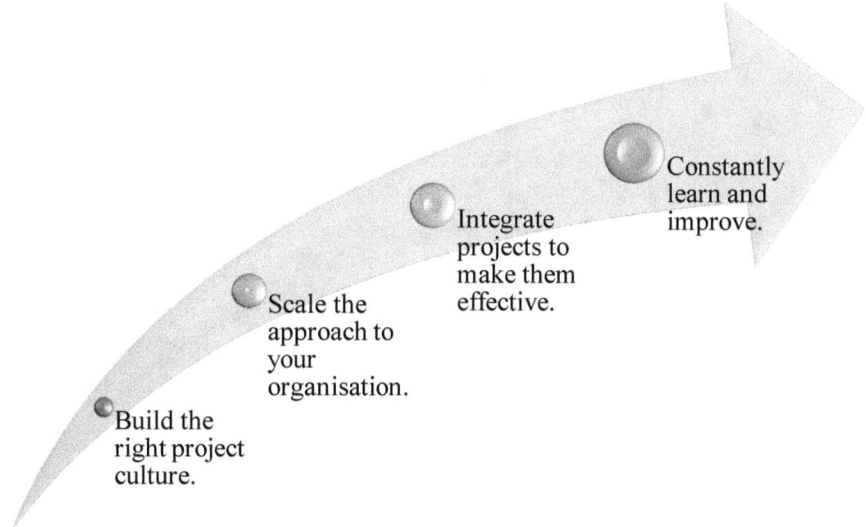

Scale the approach to your organisation.

Integrate projects to make them effective.

Constantly learn and improve.

Build the right project culture.

Figure 42- Steps to success

It's a simple message. But a simple message doesn't necessarily mean simple to implement. The themes in this book resonate with some of the fundamentals of the organisation. What is the culture? As a leader, do you have a sincere desire to adopt a project-focussed approach? Kaizen or Crisis? Building up heroes or on driving out fear? How is the company responding to change? How do you ensure tomorrow's organisation is stronger than today's?

I wish you well in leading your organization along that journey.